Treating
Opiate
Dependency

About the authors:

Donald R. Wesson, M.D., is Associate Clinical Professor, Department of Psychiatry, at the University of California, San Francisco, and is Scientific Director at Merritt Peralta Chemical Dependency Recovery Hospital in Oakland, California.

David E. Smith, M.D., is the founder and Medical Director of the Haight-Ashbury Free Medical Clinics, Research Director at the Merritt Peralta Chemical Dependency Recovery Hospital, and Associate Clinical Professor of Toxicology at the University of California, San Francisco.

Donald J. Tusel, M.D., is the Chief of the Substance Abuse Treatment Clinic at the San Francisco Veterans Administration Medical Center, and Associate Clinical Professor of Psychiatry at the University of California, San Francisco.

Treating Opiate Dependency

David E. Smith, M.D.
Donald R. Wesson, M.D.
Donald J. Tusel, M.D.

 HAZELDEN®

First published August 1989

ISBN: 0-89486-604-4

Library of Congress Catalog Card Number: 89-84201

Printed in the United States of America.

Editor's Note:

Hazelden Educational Materials offers a variety of information on chemical dependency and related areas. Our publications do not necessarily represent Hazelden or its programs, nor do they officially speak for any Twelve Step organization.

CONTENTS

Chapter

TABLES AND FIGURES

Table

Figure

ACKNOWLEDGMENTS

The authors acknowledge the contribution of the Substance Abuse Fellows at the San Francisco Veterans Administration Medical Center, Drs. Joel Nathan, Karen Sees, Robert Daigle, and Ben Carey, and the director of the fellowship program, Dr. Peter Banys, who critiqued chapters of the book and offered many valuable suggestions, additions, and corrections. Susan Camber, the Research Coordinator at Merritt Peralta Institute, contributed much to the readability of this book through her editorial advice and recommendations about structure and organization of material.

INTRODUCTION

Most Americans equate opiate dependence with heroin addiction, and the image of the heroin addict triggers one of the most negative stereotypes in our culture.[1] The heroin stereotype portrays addicts as uneducated, unemployable criminals who commit robberies or burglaries to support a deplorable, self-indulgent habit. The stereotype further assumes poor parental relationships, child abuse, or absent parents, and the addict's family is often viewed as causing, or at least enabling, the addict's misconduct.

In reality, this stereotype applies only to a subgroup of heroin addicts who are highly visible to the public treatment sector and criminal justice system. Some heroin abusers are middle class and support their opiate abuse through legitimate means.

Further, not all opiate dependence is heroin dependence. Opiate-dependent persons also include prescription drug abusers and health professionals who abuse meperidine (Demerol), fentanyl (Sublimaze), and other narcotics diverted from medical sources.

Understanding and differentiating these different subgroups of opiate-dependent persons is important, because each needs different drug control policies, prevention strategies, and treatment techniques. For example, an outreach approach effective in reaching lower socioeconomic heroin addicts congregated in a drug culture will not reach middle-class heroin-dependent people, opiate-dependent health professionals, or middle- and upper-class prescription opiate abusers. Some treatments, such as methadone maintenance, are the only forms of outpatient treatment acceptable to many street heroin addicts. On the other hand, treatment programs that use naltrexone are more acceptable to middle- and upper-class narcotic abusers, unlike traditional therapeutic communities or programs that use methadone.

1

The impact on society of opiate dependency for one population of abusers may not apply to another. For example, the high cost of heroin drives addicts to commit property crimes or deal drugs to support their drug-abusing lifestyle. But opiate-abusing health professionals who obtain their opiates by diversion from medical sources are not driven to commit property crimes to purchase opiates.

The failure to recognize the multifaceted nature of opiate dependence has hampered both prevention efforts and the development of treatment services.

AN OVERVIEW OF OPIATE DEPENDENCE

After the introduction of the hypodermic needle during the Civil War, morphinism became known as "the soldier's disease" because many men became morphine addicts during treatment of their war injuries. Opiates were also commonly available in patent medicines. At the turn of the century, most opiate-dependent people were women who became dependent by using patent medications containing opium.

Growing concern over the addiction potential of the opiates, especially heroin, coupled with media coverage of addiction and crime in minority populations, led to passage of the Harrison Narcotic Act in 1914. As a result of this and later court decisions, all opiate-dependent persons became criminals, as did the physicians who prescribed opiates to addicts as treatment for their addiction.[2] Before 1960, imprisonment was the dominant "treatment" of opiate addiction. In the 1930s, the federal government built prisons in Lexington, Kentucky and Fort Worth, Texas for treatment of opiate addicts.

Therapeutic communities were the first alternative to imprisonment for opiate addicts. The first therapeutic community to work extensively with opiate addicts was Synanon, started in California in 1959 by Charles Dederick. Although Dederick, a recovering alcoholic, incorporated many

principles of Alcoholics Anonymous (AA) into the community, he and many early leaders in therapeutic communities viewed alcoholics and heroin addicts as "different species."[3]
The founders of Synanon believed that the opiate addict must be permanently sequestered from the society that lead to addiction and that lifelong residence in a therapeutic community was necessary to prevent relapse.[4] In its early days, Synanon was viewed as an alternative culture, not as a step in rehabilitation with the goal of eventual return to mainstream society.

In New York, another therapeutic community, Daytop Lodge,* was established on Staten Island in 1963. Like Synanon, Daytop Lodge accepted court referrals and was an alternative to incarceration.[5]

The first outpatient treatment programs to which the courts referred addicts used methadone maintenance, which evolved as a treatment modality in the mid-1960s.

The treatment approaches for opiate addiction and alcoholism developed in remarkable isolation from each other. Historically, physicians characterized both alcoholism and opiate dependency as diseases. But during the dominance of the criminal justice approach to opiate addiction, few physicians treated alcoholism or opiate addiction. By the 1950s, organized medicine needed outside help in reclaiming the disease models of drug dependency. Alcoholics Anonymous, which began in 1935, established specific Steps designed to guide a person toward living a comfortable and responsible life without the use of alcohol, while remaining in a culture where alcohol was generally available. As a result of AA's insistence on calling alcoholism a disease and the American Medical Association's pronouncement in 1956 of alcoholism as a disease, the treatment of alcoholism has become more closely associated with health care delivery.

---

*DAYTOP is an acronym for Drug Addiction Treatment of Probationers.

In the 1950s, Narcotics Anonymous (NA), patterned on AA, began a movement that challenged the notion that opiate-dependent persons could not recover and live a drug-free life while living in mainstream society.

Vietnam Era Addict

The use of opium and heroin by U.S. troops in Vietnam altered society's perception of both heroin dependency and society's obligation to provide treatment for heroin addicts. Relying on the criminal justice approach was acceptable to mainstream society when it applied to unpopular minority groups, but imprisonment was politically unfashionable when the abusers happened to be veterans whose first exposure to opiates was in a controversial war. Drug-abuse experts were at first concerned that exposure of many soldiers to potent, inexpensive heroin in Southeast Asia would lead to high rates of opiate addiction in veterans after their return to the United States. The problem proved to be less severe than anticipated.

In a follow-up of veterans who had used heroin in Vietnam, Robbins et al. found that 56 percent abstained from heroin completely, 32 percent used heroin but did not become addicted, and 12 percent became re-addicted during the three years after their return to the United States.[6] Of veterans who continued heroin use after returning to the states, most had a history of drug abuse or addiction *before* they were sent to Vietnam. The Vietnam experience put into perspective the importance of the context of use, the mode of use, and preexisting drug abuse. Accessibility is important in initiating drug use, but a susceptible host is a significant factor in developing and sustaining addiction.

Partially as a counterculture backlash to the Vietnam war, many middle-class youths established a new drug-using subculture during the sixties. In the Haight-Ashbury section of San Francisco in 1968 and 1969, for example, many amphetamine abusers first used barbiturates and other sedatives and later heroin to reduce unwanted symptoms of their amphetamine abuse. This upper-downer cycle often resulted in secondary dependence on heroin.

By the early seventies, heroin had become acceptable to some members of this new subculture. By that time, reliance on the criminal justice system to deal with middle class youth and young adults was losing hold. The federal government, through the Special Action Office on Drug Abuse Prevention, established a network of drug treatment clinics throughout the country. The treatment approach was justified politically because of the relationship between heroin addiction and crime. The slogan that "No addict should have to commit a crime because of inability to receive treatment" received widespread political endorsement.

During the eighties, the upper-downer cycles seen with amphetamines repeated with increasing abuse of cocaine, another potent central nervous system psychostimulant. Smoking cocaine free-base became popular among people who were not needle-using, hard-core drug abusers. Some people who used cocaine free-base combined it with Persian heroin (free-base heroin). Free-base heroin was smoked with, or just after, smoking cocaine free-base. Although this pattern of abuse developed among people who initially were not needle-users, some began using needles as their dependence on heroin increased, because intravenous injection is a more efficient way of using heroin.

Opiate Addiction Among Health Professionals

Both professional licensing boards and the general public are becoming increasingly aware of opiate dependency among nurses, physicians, veterinarians, pharmacists, and dentists. They all have access in the workplace to pharmaceutically manufactured opiates: morphine, meperidine (Demerol), and fentanyl. The public's awareness of drug use by health professionals is, in part, due to increased sensitivity about drug use

5

in the workplace. But the awareness also reflects a probable increase in frequency of opiate abuse among health professionals, particularly among younger health professionals. Before entering professional training, many of them used marijuana, amphetamines, and a broader range of recreational drugs than did previous generations. Once within the medical profession, however, they usually go to great lengths to hide their narcotic use from their peers.

The New Wave: Opiate Dependency in the 1980s

Three new ripples on the surface of opiate dependency are particularly disturbing.

First, designer opiates (explored in greater detail in Chapter One) can be domestically synthesized in clandestine laboratories; this will undermine efforts to limit heroin availability through international treaties and interdiction of supplies entering the country.

Second, cocaine abuse, which has emerged as the major illicit drug problem of the 1980s, is undermining the social benefit of methadone maintenance. Cocaine has always been popular among heroin users, but its present widespread availability and popularity are unprecedented. Many methadone maintenance patients who no longer use heroin, but who continue to use cocaine, engage in a high level of criminal activity because the cost of cocaine is similar to that of heroin. Further, since cocaine induces paranoia and psychoses that are detrimental to the patients and the treatment milieu, its use by patients enrolled in methadone maintenance clinics is particularly disruptive.

Finally, the association of HIV infection with intravenous drug use has profound implications for the opiate-dependent individual. Because the heroin addict has been perceived as the vector of HIV infection to the heterosexual population, there have been increases in federal resources for AIDS research

ADDICTION TREATMENT CENTER

At Prince William Hospital

8680 Hospital Way • Manassas, Virginia 22110
(703) 369-8464 • Metro 631-1750

among intravenous drug users and increases in the funding of drug treatment, particularly methadone maintenance.

Heroin Use in Other Countries

Heroin abuse is, of course, not limited to the United States. In some countries, government response, treatment systems, and self-help groups have taken a substantially different course than that taken in the United States. For example, in large cities in the Netherlands, methadone is dispensed to addict clients from a mobile bus that comes to specific locations at specified times.[7] The mobile treatment reduces the number of methadone clinics needed and thus eases the concerns of people who do not want methadone maintenance clinics located in their neighborhoods. Mobile dispensing also breaks up the congregation of addicts that methadone clinics foster.

Unlike in the United States, heroin addicts in the Netherlands are politically active. United under the Federation of Dutch Junkie Leagues, representatives meet with the legislators about matters affecting the users of heroin, such as distribution of methadone and free clean syringes, the policy of lawmakers and police, and housing problems. The Junkie League also publishes a periodical describing the activities of the league, the experiences of addicts, and an analysis of heroin use information in the popular media. The Junkie League actively promotes the interests of heroin users.[8]

Medical Treatment of Pain and Opiate Dependence

The current concern about opiate dependence is significantly affecting the way pain patients are treated. Treating chronic pain with narcotics arouses professional controversy and frequent clinical concern. Opiates are still the most appropriate medications for management of severe pain. Chronic pain patients who take opiates develop tolerance and physical dependence that may be mistaken for addiction. Addiction specialists may be consulted to assess the patient's addiction,[9] and we have seen instances where chronic pain patients were inappropriately treated for chemical dependency.

In the chronic pain patient, the distinction between appropriate medical use of an opiate and opiate dependency rests not on physical dependence, tolerance, and regular use, but on *maladaptive behavioral changes* associated with opiate use. The changes would include, for example, escalation of dose without the physician's knowledge or concurrence, or obtaining opiates from several physcians without disclosing the fact to the physicians.

Substance abuse and dependency criteria have been changed in the *Diagnostic and Statistical Manual of Mental Disorders, Third Edition, Revised (DSM-III-R)*[10] to emphasize clinically significant maladaptive behaviors associated with drug abuse and dependence. The criteria for dependence, for example, will work for "opiate dependence" even in the presence of high-dose, regular opiate use. Tolerance and physical dependence alone do not establish a diagnosis of "opiate dependence." The person must also show maladaptive behavior in relation to the opiate use. For example, "important social, occupational, or recreational activities given up or reduced because of the opiate use" or "continued substance use despite knowledge of having a persistent or recurrent social, psychological, or physical problem that is caused or exacerbated by the use of the substance."[11] Unless maladaptive behaviors of chronic pain patients are driven by their opiate use, addiction treatment is not appropriate for them. Although many physicians under-medicate acute pain with opiates because of concern about producing opiate dependency, most physicians are inadequately informed about the risk of prescribing even small amounts of opiates to individuals who are recovering from opiate dependency. Thus, many patients recovering from opiate addiction are still being inappropriately treated by physicians who do not understand that even small amounts of prescribed opiates can precipitate drug hunger and a relapse to opiate abuse. Although there are alternatives to opiates as a means of pain control, they aren't used because the alternatives are more expensive and time consuming, and because opiates are the standard medical treatment. Recovering patients can take an active role by informing their physicians about their addiction history, their desire for alternative treatments, and if necessary, find physicians who will work with them to minimize the risk of relapse.

OPIATE USE AND CRIME

An important stimulus for federal funding of drug-abuse treatment in the early 1970s was the association between heroin addiction and crime. DuPont and Green described an increase in crime in Washington, D.C. that paralleled the prevalence of heroin addiction.[12] They also noted a strong inverse relationship between the number of patients in treatment and the property crime rate. Thus, much of the support for opiate treatment reflected the hope that treatment would reduce crime.

Crime is linked to heroin dependence because of the high cost of heroin, rather than the heroin use *per se*. The price is supported by its illegality and the government's interdiction of supply. This has spurred debates about the legalization of drugs, including heroin.

Advocates for legalization argue that because the enormous profits in the drug trade would be wiped out, smugglers' incentives to bring heroin into the country would be reduced, user cost lowered, and arrests for drug possession eliminated. Lower cost and legal availability would greatly reduce, if not eliminate, the need for addicts to commit property crimes to purchase heroin. With drugs available through legal channels, quality could be controlled, and medical complications resulting from using contaminated drugs and unsterile needles would be eliminated. They also argue that criminalization hasn't worked in spite of huge expenditures of public funds and that the current policy of allowing legal use of certain drugs (alcohol and nicotine) while criminalizing the use of others is irrational.

Those opposed to legalization point out that our biggest drug problem is alcohol, a drug that is legal, and that even more people would abuse drugs if the medical dangers of drug use and the price of drugs were reduced. To some extent, drug use and the choice of drugs used is determined by availability. If drugs such as heroin were legalized, much of the social cost would remain, but it would be shifted to other resources, such as those needed to treat increased numbers of people who would become dependent.

Opiate dependence in some groups is not associated with increased property crime. For example, as stated earlier, no causal relationship exists between opiate dependency and property crime among health professionals.

CHANGING TREATMENT MODALITIES

The three major treatment modalities for heroin abuse — methadone maintenance, therapeutic community, and drug-free recovery — evolved separately. Although methadone maintenance had its genesis in the medical model of treatment, its popularity as a treatment modality was driven mainly by crime prevention. Therapeutic communities were an adaptation of techniques developed for the treatment of the mentally ill, blended with concepts from AA. NA, of course, had its origins in AA.

Because of different traditions and underlying philosophies, substantial conflict exists between the modalities. For example, NA, developing from the tradition of AA, emphasizes abstinence from all drugs. Within early therapeutic communities, however, the use of alcohol was perceived as a necessary social skill. The need for abstinence from alcohol was not stressed, and drinking privileges were used as a reward for progress in the program.[13] Likewise, in methadone maintenance, most effort was expended on controlling drugs such as heroin, cocaine, and amphetamine, while alcohol and marijuana use was tolerated.

Failure to stress abstinence from alcohol has had major consequences for therapeutic communities and methadone maintenance. Many therapeutic community graduates and early leaders of therapeutic communities have themselves subsequently developed alcoholism. In some methadone-maintenance clinics, alcohol-induced cirrhosis of the liver is a leading cause of death.

The 1980s have brought a trend toward the integration of a drug-free philosophy into therapeutic communities and methadone maintenance. This is an important advance. Without a drug-free philosophy of treatment, the addict often shifts from abuse of one substance to another.

Outpatient treatment for alcoholism and all other forms of drug dependency is becoming more common too. Therapeutic communities and halfway houses are now seen as steps toward the return to community-based treatment.

Inpatient treatment of opiate dependence in the private sector evolved from recovery-oriented treatment of alcoholism, just as NA is an adaptation of AA. Over time, they have become better organized with programs and goals clearly delineated. Inpatient treatment practices have been codified by the Joint Commission on Accreditation of Hospitals. In addition, most states have departments of alcohol and drug abuse that issue regulations that must be followed for inpatient drug abuse treatment programs and outpatient drug abuse treatment clinics. Insurance reimbursement practices have also had a significant influence on how drug abuse treatment is structured.

Government regulations, particularly with regard to methadone, and more recently with inpatient treatment, have played a role in freezing clinical practices, program policies, and procedures. Methadone-detoxification and methadone-maintenance clinics are regulated by two federal agencies: the federal

Food and Drug Administration and the Drug Enforcement Administration. Further, state regulatory agencies, which usually have more restrictive regulations than the federal agencies, also oversee the operations of methadone-maintenance clinics.

AIDS AND DRUG ABUSE

The growing crisis with AIDS and its association with intravenous drug abuse is again refocusing the goals of treatment. Of the 49,515 cases of AIDS reported to the Center for Disease Control in Atlanta, 8,511 (17 percent) were in I.V. drug abusers. Another 3,726 (8 percent) cases were both homosexual *and* I.V. drug abusers.[14] A few years before, the major cause of death among heroin addicts was violence and overdose; now, AIDS is a major cause of death among I.V. narcotic addicts.

In this environment, the emphasis of treatment becomes stopping I.V. drug use and needle-sharing. Substitution of other modes of use, such as smoking by the addict, while undesirable, is tolerated. In response to the spread of AIDS among drug abusers who share needles, many states are expanding methadone maintenance. Because of rapid expansion, methadone maintenance is not necessarily part of an integrated treatment program, a considerable concern to those who direct well-run, comprehensive methadone maintenance programs.

A number of new controversial techniques for containing the HIV infection are now being advocated: quarantine of HIV-positive people, incarceration, and needle exchange programs. In San Francisco, the Haight-Ashbury Free Medical Clinics, in association with the Mid-City Consortium, is using community health outreach workers to pass out information about drug treatment resources, along with bottles of bleach to be used in sterilizing needles. Particularly targeted are high-risk minority and gay drug abusers.

While the AIDS epidemic has focused public attention on

the opiate addict and the opiate addict's threat to the broader society, the response to opiate addiction may differ from that of previous decades. New drug treatment capabilities have developed during the past twenty years, and many drug treatment clinics and programs are now in place.

Professional response may also be different. The uninterrupted public support for drug treatment, along with the development of many private inpatient drug treatment programs, has decreased the stigma of treating drug dependency. The American Medical Society for the Treatment of Alcoholism and Other Drug Dependencies (AMSAODD), a national organization consisting of physicians who have interest in the treatment of chemical dependency, now has over three thousand physician members. With the backing of large professional organizations, physicians treating opiate addiction are now much less likely to be criminalized and stigmatized. Both the AMA's position and the revised criteria for substance abuse disorders in *DSM-III-R* have helped unify alcohol and substance abuse treatment.

Finally, the president's AIDS Commission of 1988 recommended a rapid expansion of drug treatment for I.V. drug abusers. This contrasts to recommendations of previous commissions that favored stronger law enforcement.

NEUROBIOLOGY OF ADDICTION

Since the first demonstration of opiate receptors[15] in nervous tissue in 1973, scientists have learned much about the neurobiology of opiate dependence. Nonetheless, except for clonidine detoxification and naltrexone treatment, this knowledge has not yet resulted in significant changes in treating opiate-dependent people. As this knowledge is translated into new treatments, clinicians will need to better understand physiological recovery as well as psychological recovery from opiate dependence.

We included the neurobiology of addiction in this book

because we have found that most nonmedical treatment personnel are interested in knowing about endorphins and receptors and their relevance for treatment. But information is still hard to obtain because it is incomprehensible as found in the medical and scientific literature. We have tried in this book to summarize this material and make it understandable to both medical and nonmedical chemical dependency treatment staff.

Opiate abuse in the United States in 1988 is more diverse and complicated than in previous decades. The treatment options, ranging from drug-maintenance to drug-free, have increased, and interactions between treatment systems have become more complicated. We hope that this book, which integrates current theory and practice related to treatment of opiate abuse, will benefit those who want to understand better the nature of opiate addiction and the many recent advances that have been made in its treatment. Scientists have learned more about brain chemistry in the past twenty years than they have in the entire preceding history of science, and these advances have profound implications for both treatment and public policy. We have tried to summarize for physicians, counselors, and other substance-abuse specialists clinically relevant scientific findings and new knowledge about street opiates and patterns of abuse, and present an overview of ideas about treatment of opiate dependency. We have also tried to provide details of pharmacological treatment in sufficient depth to be of practical value to physicians.

Introduction
ENDNOTES

1. J. J. Platt, *Heroin Addiction: Theory, Research, and Treatment,* 2nd ed. (Malabar, Fla.: Krieger, 1986), 165.
2. Ibid., 22.
3. J. E. Zweben and D. E. Smith, "Changing Attitudes and Policies toward Alcohol Use in the Therapeutic Community," *Journal of Psychoactive Drugs* 18 (1986): 253-60.

4. M. S. Cherkas, "Synanon Foundation — A Radical Approach to the Problem of Addiction," *American Journal of Psychiatry* 121 (1965): 1065-69.
5. D. A. Deitch, "Treatment of Drug Abuse in the Therapeutic Community: Historical Influences, Current Considerations and Future Outlook," in *Drug Abuse in America*, vol. IV (Washington, D.C.: National Commission on Marijuana and Drug Abuse, 1973): 158-75.
6. L. N. Robbins, "Addict Careers," *Handbook on Drug Abuse*, R. I. DuPont, A. Goldstein, and J. O'Donnel, eds. (Washington, D.C.: National Institute on Drug Abuse, 1979): 325-36.
7. G. F. van de Wijngaart, "Heroin use in the Netherlands," *American Journal of Drug and Alcohol Abuse* 14 (1988): 125-36.
8. Ibid., 130.
9. H. W. Clark and K. L. Sees, "Chronic Pain and the Chemical Dependency Specialist," *California Society for the Treatment of Alcoholism and Other Drug Dependencies NEWS* 15 (1988): 1-9.
10. *Diagnostic and Statistical Manual of Mental Disorders*, Third Edition, Revised (Washington, D.C.: American Psychiatric Association, 1987), 165-85.
11. Ibid., 168.
12. R. L. DuPont and H. M. Green, "The Dynamics of Heroin Addiction Epidemic," *Science* 181 (1973): 716-22.
13. Zweben and Smith, "Changing Attitudes and Policies," 254.
14. "Update: Acquired Immunodeficiency Syndrome (AIDS) — Worldwide," *Journal of the American Medical Association* 259 (21) (1988): 3104-7.
15. C. B. Pert and S. H. Snyder, "Opiate Receptor: Demonstration in Nervous Tissue," *Science* 179 (1973): 1011-14.

1
OPIATE DRUGS

TERMINOLOGY

Some of the terminology that refers to opiate drugs can be confusing, for example, the terms *opiate* and *opioid*. Traditional pharmacology designates compounds that are derived from opium, such as morphine and heroin, as *opiates*. Compounds with similar pharmacological properties that are partially or completely synthesized in a pharmaceutical laboratory, such as meperidine (Demerol) or methadone are called *opioids*.

With the discovery of an opiate receptor that bonds to morphine, compounds that bond to the opiate receptor and produced morphine-like effects were termed *opioid agonist* and compounds that block the opioid agonist, such as naloxone (Narcan) or naltrexone (Trexan) were called *opioid antagonist*. In these cases, the terms *opiate* and *opioid* are used interchangeably.

With the discovery of multiple opiate receptors, endogenous opiates, such as endorphins, and synthetically produced compounds with mixed antagonist effects, such as pentazocine (Talwin), and buprenorphine (Temgesic), have made the terminology even more confusing. Some authors use the term opioid to refer to all exogenous compounds that bind to any of the opiate receptors and produce agonist effects.[1] In this book, we use the terms *opiate* and *opioid* interchangeably, and we include all drugs that are abused for morphine-like effects.

Maximum Strength and Milligram Strength

Potency is another term subject to confusion because it can

have two different meanings: maximum strength and milligram strength. Maximum strength refers to the largest amount of pain that an opiate can relieve. Using the maximum strength definition, morphine, for example, can relieve more pain than codeine because morphine will relieve pain of greater intensity than codeine.

Milligram strength compares the painkilling effects of a drug to a particular amount of morphine. When we say, for example, that fentanyl is eighty times as potent as morphine, we do not mean that fentanyl will relieve a greater amount of pain than morphine, but rather that a 1 mg dose of fentanyl will relieve the same amount of pain as an 80 mg dose of morphine. In this book, potency will refer to milligram potency unless otherwise specified.

Where Opiates Come From

Opiates come from three sources:

1. The poppy, *Papaver somniferum,* is the source of opium, the raw material for codeine, morphine, and heroin, and is the main source of illicit opiates.
2. Synthesis in pharmaceutical laboratories and diversion from medicinal sources to street use is another source.
3. There are chemists who produce designer illicit opiates. While presently small producers, these chemists are potentially a major source of illicit opiates.

Most of the opium that finds its way to the illicit drug market is grown in either Southeast Asia (Burma, Laos, Thailand, and Vietnam), Southwest Asia (Iran, Afghanistan, and Pakistan), or Mexico.

International efforts to control opiate availability by controlling growing of the opium-producing poppy have met with mixed results. Governments of some countries have cooperated with international drug control and are no longer major sources of opium for the illicit drug market, but new production has begun in many other countries.

THE OPIUM-PRODUCING POPPY

Opium is obtained from the milky fluid that oozes from incisions made in poppy pods before they discharge seeds. The fluid is scraped from the pod by hand and air dried, producing opium. This substance is comprised of 4 to 21 percent morphine, 1 to 2.5 percent codeine, and approximately twenty other alkaloids, some of which have medicinal uses.

To facilitate smuggling from growing areas, opium is usually converted to morphine base, which results in about a tenfold reduction in bulk and makes transport easier. Later, morphine base is converted to heroin.

SYNTHETICS AND SEMISYNTHETICS

Opiates that are made by chemical manipulations of ingredients of opium are called *semisynthetics.* Those that are made without starting from opium derivatives are called *synthetics.*

Heroin

Heroin does not naturally occur in opium, but is easily produced from morphine. Heroin was first made from morphine in 1874 (commercial production of heroin by the Bayer Company in Germany began in 1898). Around the turn of the century, heroin was used in the United States as a treatment for morphinism (morphine-dependence).

Pure heroin is a white powder with a bitter taste. Illicit heroin is often brown or black because of impurities left from the manufacturing process or the presence of additives. Southeast Asian heroin is produced in two ways. One process produces heroin with a purity range of 70 to 95 percent; this is referred to by the Drug Enforcement Administration as heroin number 4. The other processing method, resulting in heroin with a purity range of 20 to 40 percent, is called heroin number 3, and is produced primarily for smoking in Southeast Asia.[2] Mexican heroin is usually sold on the street, either as a brown powder, with a purity of 3 to 10 percent, or as "black tar," which may contain 20 to 80 percent heroin.

Heroin is commonly sold to the user in 100 mg bags, containing on an average, about 5 mg of heroin and 95 mg sugar, starch, powdered milk, or quinine.

Hydromorphone

Hydromorphone (Dilaudid) is a semisynthetic opiate. Physicians prescribe Dilaudid for treatment of severe pain. It is available in tablets (1, 2, and 4 mg), powder (1000 mg vials), ampules for injection (1, 2, 4 and 10 mg/ml), and rectal suppositories (3 mg/suppository). It is also available in syrup (1 mg hydromorphone/5 ml) for cough suppression.

Dilaudid on the illicit drug market has been diverted from medical channels, most often in 2 or 4 mg tablets. Opiate addicts often acquire Dilaudid by going to physicians or to emergency rooms where they complain of pain and obtain a prescription, or by seeing a physician who sells prescriptions, known as a "scrip doc."

Dilaudid powder, marketed to hospital pharmacies, has been diverted from medical sources, mixed with quinine, and sold on the streets as heroin. In Washington, D.C., for example, twelve Dilaudid overdose deaths occurred within a two week period in September 1987.[3] The victims were opiate addicts who injected Dilaudid powder believing it to be heroin. This was an unusually high rate of Dilaudid overdoses.

Oxycodone

Oxycodone is a semisynthetic that is made from thebaine, one of the alkaloids in opium. It is marketed in combination

with aspirin as Percodan, or in combination with acetaminophen (whose brand name is Tylenol) as Percocet, Tylox, or
Vicodan. Addicts abusing oxycodone usually inject it intra-
muscularly. The combinations are irritating to tissues and
often result in scarring and abscesses at the injection sites.

Meperidine

Meperidine, brand name Demerol, is a synthetic opiate,
commonly administered in hospitals for pain control. Demerol
is available as a tablet for oral administration. It is, however,
usually administered by injection because Demerol tablets are
unreliably absorbed.

Among opiates, Demerol has the unusual characteristic of
producing grand mal seizures at high doses. It is not widely
available on the street, but it is the most commonly abused
opiate by nurses and other health professionals, except for
anesthesiologists, who usually abuse fentanyl.

Fentanyl

Fentanyl is a synthetic opiate developed by Janssen Pharmaceuticals in 1952. It is used in the United States as an adjunct
to anesthesia and is available only in ampules for injection
under the trade names of Innovar or Sublimaze. Its milligram
potency as a painkiller is about 80 times that of morphine. It
is a common drug of abuse by anesthesiologists and other
operating room personnel.

Clinical trials are being conducted using transdermal
patches as a way of delivering fentanyl for postoperative pain.
Its high-milligram potency makes this mode of delivery practical. The transdermal patch will eliminate or reduce the need
for intramuscular injections of opiates for pain control. If the
transdermal patch becomes incorporated into routine clinical
practice, it is likely to become a significant drug of abuse by

medical personnel because of the ease of application and concealment.

Fentanyl and its analogues are abused by street addicts as heroin substitutes under the street name of *China White*. Fentanyl that is available to the street addict is illicitly manufactured.

Detection of Fentanyl Analogues in Urine

Although radioimmunoassay techniques can detect fentanyl and its analogues in urine, they are not usually detected in common drug screening. Addicts using fentanyl analogues may not have detectable opiates in their urine even when they are using them on a daily basis. This, of course, invalidates urine testing as a means of reliably detecting relapse in addicts in treatment, and — as will be subsequently discussed in the chapter on methadone maintenance — complicates the assessment of eligibility for methadone maintenance treatment.

Methadone

Methadone, first synthesized by German scientists during World War II because of a shortage of morphine, was used in the United States as early as 1947 for pain control and has been used since the early 1960s for treatment of narcotic dependency. It is well absorbed when given orally, and it has a long duration of action, both of which make methadone a feasible substitute opiate for treatment of opiate dependence. Most patients in methadone maintenance programs need to take only one dose of methadone per day, making administration in a clinic setting practical.

Propoxyphene

Chemically, propoxyphene (Darvon) is a synthetic opiate that is similar to methadone in chemical structure, but weaker in opiate effects. It is available by medical prescription as either propoxyphene *hydrochloride* or propoxyphene *napsylate.*

- Propoxyphene hydrochloride is available alone under the trade name of Darvon. It is also available in combination with aspirin (Darvon with ASA); aspirin, phenacetin, and caffeine (Darvon Compound, SK-65); or acetaminophen (Darvocet). Propoxyphene napsylate is sold under the trade name of Darvon-N.
- Propoxyphene napsylate has been used as a treatment for heroin withdrawal. In 1980, it was rescheduled as a Schedule IV narcotic.[4] The reclassification of propoxyphene napsylate as a narcotic brings it under the Narcotics Treatment Act of 1974, restricting its use in treatment of opiate-dependent patients.

DESIGNER OPIATES

The term *designer drugs,* attributed to Dr. Gary Henderson (a professor of pharmacology at the University of California, Davis), refers to drugs that are slight chemical modifications of ones already scheduled under the Controlled Substances Act. In producing the new drugs, which are also called *drug analogues* or *congeners,* the chemist hopes to create a "not yet illegal" drug that still retains the parent drug's psychoactive properties.

Designer drugs is not a precise term, nor is its use restricted to opiate drugs. Nonopiate drugs, such as methylenedioxyamphetamine (MDA), and its analog methylenedioxymethamphetamine (MDMA, also called Ecstasy, XTC), are often called designer drugs. When applied to opiates, *designer drugs* generally refers to the analogues of fentanyl and meperidine (Demerol).

Although the term *designer drugs* is relatively new, the clandestine manufacture of analogues of controlled drugs is not. In the late 1960s, street chemists produced a number of amphetamine and mescaline analogues that became drugs of abuse.

Attention to fentanyl analogues* as drugs of abuse developed in 1980 when several unexplained deaths occurred among narcotic addicts in Southern California. Although the circumstances of the deaths suggested narcotic overdose, blood and urine tests showed no evidence of heroin or other common street narcotics.[5] Later, they were found to have overdosed on alpha-methyl fentanyl, which was sold on the streets as "China White."[6] The episode was reported in the popular press in 1981.[7]

Control of Designer Opiates

The availability of designer opiates undermines the government's efforts to limit illicit opiate availability by curtailing opium production. Designer opiates are produced domestically, and it is difficult to intercept these drugs while they are being routed from the manufacturing laboratory to the opiate addict. Thousands of doses can be concealed in a small space because of the high-milligram potency of the fentanyl analogues.

Because chemists continue to create drugs that are not yet illegal, fentanyl analogues have been the impetus for two important federal drug laws. The first, The Comprehensive Crime Control Act of 1984 (Public Law 98-473), provides, among other things, that the Drug Enforcement Administration is authorized to place drugs temporarily into Schedule I if the scheduling is necessary to avoid an imminent hazard to the public safety. The second law, The Controlled Substance Analog Enforcement Act of 1986 (Public Law 99-570), commonly

---

* Such as 2 methyl-2,5 dimethoxylamphetamine (STP) and 3,4-methylenedioxyamphetamine (MDA).

called the "designer drug" bill, was intended to allow criminal prosecution of "designer drug" chemists.

Consequences to the Opiate Addict

A severe consequence of the availability of high-potency designer drugs to the opiate addict is that the small volume of the dosage unit increases probability of overdose, and mis-synthesis may cause brain damage.

Chapter 1
ENDNOTES

1. J. H. Jaffe and W. R. Martin, "Opioid Analgesics and Antagonists," in *Goodman and Gilman's: The Pharmacological Basis of Therapeutics,* ed. A. G. Gilman, L. S. Goodman, and A. Gilman (New York: Macmillan, 1980), 494-534.
2. U.S. Department of Justice/Drug Enforcement Administration, *Intelligence Trends: From the Source to the Street: Current Prices for Cannabis, Cocaine, and Heroin,* vol. 14, no. 3 (Washington, D.C.: U.S. Government Printing Office, 1987), 9.
3. Center for Disease Control, "Dilaudid Related Deaths — District of Columbia, 1987," *Morbidity and Mortality Weekly Report* 37 (15 July 1988): 425-27.
4. *Federal Register* 45 FR 42264 (June 24, 1980).
5. T. Ziporyn, "A Growing Industry and Menace: Makeshift Laboratory's Designer Drugs," *Journal of the American Medical Association* 256 (1986): 3061-63.
6. J. L. Brittain, "China White: The Bogus Drug," *Journal of Toxicology. Clinical Toxicology* 19 (1982): 1123-26.
7. T. Morganthau, J. Contreras, and P. Abramson, "A Deadly New Drug Passing as Heroin," *Newsweek* 97 (5 January 1981): 21.

2
ASSESSMENT

Assessment is the systematic process of collecting information needed for a treatment plan to guide therapeutic interventions with the patient. This information is used in two ways:

- To identify *problems* that must be addressed during treatment.
- To identify *patient characteristics* and *resources* that can be mobilized in the service of recovery.

Each piece of information should, alone or in combination with other information, have the potential of changing the treatment strategy or interventions. During treatment, periodic assessments monitor progress and determine additional treatment interventions.

The following seven categories cover the basic information areas needed for initial treatment planning.

1. Alcohol and other drug abuse.
2. Medical problems.
3. Emotional problems.
4. Residence, family, and other social support.
5. Legal difficulties.
6. Work and use of leisure time.
7. Financial resources.

McLellan and his associates at the Veterans Administration Medical Center in Philadelphia have developed a structured interview, the Addiction Severity Index,[1] that can be administered by a trained counselor in about forty-five minutes. The structured interview, which probes each of the areas listed, is one way of systematically collecting such assessment information.

INITIAL ASSESSMENT

Alcohol and Other Drug Abuse

The patient's drug abuse history is an important tool in understanding his or her relationship to drugs and potential for rehabilitation. A polydrug abuser, for example, who indiscriminately abuses different classes of drugs simultaneously, is generally a poor candidate for drug-class specific treatment, such as methadone maintenance.

Information should be collected not only about periods of drug use, but periods of abstinence from alcohol or other drugs. One wants to know how abstinence was achieved and maintained and what life circumstances lead to abstinence.

The circumstances of relapse should be determined because these circumstances are vulnerable points for future relapses. If possible, the patient's environment should be restructured to avoid situations in which relapse occurred. If the situations can't be avoided, the counselor and patient should agree on a plan for coping with such situations (also see relapse prevention in Chapter Seven). The patient's acceptance of, prior attendance at, and familiarity with Twelve Step recovery groups, such as Narcotics Anonymous or Alcoholics Anonymous, are important to ascertain. If the person is not familiar with them, he or she should be informed about Twelve Step recovery and begin attending a number of meetings. If the patient has attended Twelve Step meetings in the past, but rejected Twelve Step work, the counselor should explore the reasons.

The relationship of one kind of drug use to another is also important; for example, does the patient increase alcohol or marijuana use when opiates are not available?

Some opiate addicts will abuse alcohol to such an extent that an additional diagnosis of alcohol dependence is warranted. Since withdrawal from large quantities of alcohol (or other sedative-hypnotics) can be life threatening, withdrawal should generally be done in a hospital.

Medical Problems

Opiate addicts neglect their health and may have serious undiagnosed infections or chronic disease. Drug abuse treatment provides an opportunity to identify serious medical problems. Medical assessment should include a medical history, physical examination, and screening laboratory tests, such as a complete blood count (which checks the red and white blood cells), a panel of tests to check the function of liver and kidneys, and infectious diseases including hepatitis and AIDS. A chest X-ray is desirable to make certain the patient does not have communicable diseases such as tuberculosis.

Emotional Problems

A number of psychometric instruments have been used in clinical practice and research studies for assessing the psychological status of drug abusers. A word of caution, however: neither psychometric instruments nor clinical assessment is completely satisfactory for drug abusers who are *currently using drugs,* are in *withdrawal,* or are in *early abstinence.* Assessing psychiatric disorders among opiate-dependent patients, particularly those who also abuse alcohol, cocaine, amphetamine, psychedelics, or PCP, is difficult because the drugs may cause many symptoms of schizophrenia or major affective disorders. The difficulty in establishing psychiatric diagnoses in close proximity to drug abuse may partly explain the divergent figures that are reported in the substance abuse literature about the prevalence of psychiatric illness among heroin addicts.

Most psychiatric symptoms occurring during drug abuse or early abstinence improve with time without specific psychiatric treatment. Sometimes, however, an individual's emotional problems, such as depression or schizophrenia, become more pronounced with drug abstinence, particularly if the person is a heroin abuser, because heroin use may mask symptoms.

Early psychiatric assessment should determine whether the patient is actively suicidal or homicidal, or whether a psychosis exists that would preclude treatment outside of a psychiatric hospital. After the patient has detoxified and achieved several weeks of abstinence, a more complete psychiatric assessment can determine whether medication treatment of an underlying affective disorder, schizophrenia, or anxiety disorder is indicated.

Residence, Family, and Other Social Support

A patient's living environment influences the type of treatment that is needed. A person who lives with other drug abusers or lives in an environment that does not support recovery is unlikely to remain abstinent.

A patient's family can either undermine treatment or support sobriety. Assessing the patient's family will help to identify the treatment services needed by family members to support the patient's abstinence. The assessment may answer these questions:

- How has the drug use affected interpersonal and family interactions?
- Should family members be involved in early treatment?

Often it is a family crisis that causes a patient to seek treatment. The program's timely and effective intervention can be important in holding the patient in treatment.

Legal Difficulties

An opiate addict rarely applies for treatment without legal entanglements, such as a pending arraignment or probation hearing. Legal problems may positively influence the patient's participation in treatment, or they can be a barrier to treatment; for example, some therapeutic communities will not accept clients with pending court dates.

Resolution of the legal problems often requires treatment staff to write letters or reports for a court, probation officer, or parole officer. The counselor should be very specific about the information he or she is willing to give to the court and make certain the patient has signed the necessary authorizations for release of information before any information transfer takes place.

Work and Use of Leisure Time

A heroin addict's day is mostly spent obtaining resources to purchase heroin and using it. Following entry into treatment and early abstinence, the addict will have a large amount of unstructured time available. Restructuring this time into activities supportive of recovery is an important task early in treatment. Later, after the psychosocial crises that brought the addict to treatment have stabilized, and after abstinence is achieved, additional assessment is needed. This includes assessing the patient's educational and vocational goals, as well as the person's finances and leisure activities.

Financial Resources

It is important to examine the patient's financial resources to determine what treatment options are available. This would include disability insurance, cash on hand, and potential earning ability.

TREATMENT PROGRESS

After the patient has been in treatment for a period of time, the focus of his or her treatment may change as a result of new information, changes in the patient's lifestyle, or progress in treatment. As described in Chapter Five on methadone maintenance, federal Food and Drug Administration regulations mandate that patients' methadone maintenance treatment plans be revised every three months during the first year of treatment.

Chapter 2
ENDNOTE

1. A. T. McLellan, L. Luborsky, J. Caciola, et al., *Guide to the Addiction Severity Index: Background, Administration, and Field Testing.*

3
DRUG-FREE TREATMENT OF
OPIATE DEPENDENTS

Abstinence from opiates and all other mood-altering drugs is the primary therapeutic goal of drug-free treatment modalities. This contrasts with the goal of pharmacotherapeutic-maintenance approaches — such as methadone maintenance — in which reduction of criminal behavior and improvement of psychosocial function are the primary concerns.

The distinction between the drug-free and drug-maintenance approaches does not hinge on whether the patient is taking medications. Many drug-free programs encourage the use of disulfiram (Antabuse) to prevent relapse to alcohol abuse, or naltrexone (Trexan) to prevent relapse to opiate abuse. Psychotherapeutic medications — such as lithium or antidepressants — are allowed when indicated for treatment of an underlying psychiatric disturbance. As a matter of philosophy, however, staff working in drug-free programs would not endorse the use of methadone by someone being treated for opiate dependency, nor would most drug-free programs approve of a patient taking a medication with substantial abuse potential — a sleeping pill or tranquilizer, such as diazepam (Valium), chlordiazepoxide (Librium), or alprazolam (Xanax).

Drug-free treatment may be provided in inpatient drug-abuse treatment programs, social model residential programs, outpatient drug abuse treatment programs, community mental health clinics, or therapeutic communities. Some drug-free treatment programs (for example, inpatient chemical dependency recovery hospitals and social model residential treatment) use treatment as an introduction to Twelve Step recovery processes. Other types of drug-free treatment approaches (mental health clinics with a drug-abuse treatment component) rely primarily on individual and group psychotherapy.

In this chapter, we will describe the major drug-free treatment and recovery modalities for opiate-dependent patients, emphasizing their origin, their conflicts with other treatments, and recent trends. We use the term *recovery* to refer to the process of learning to live a comfortable and responsible life without the use of psychoactive drugs. Most commonly, recovery includes participation in the Twelve Step recovery group process, but it should be recognized that Twelve Step participation is not the *only* path to recovery.

CHEMICAL DEPENDENCY TREATMENT

Hospital-Based Inpatient Programs

Many hospital-based chemical dependency programs treat opiate-dependent patients. Most of these inpatient drug treatment programs evolved from the twenty-eight day alcohol inpatient treatment programs. Typically, the programs provide medically supervised detoxification, individual and group counseling, and participation in Twelve Step programs.[1]

Medical insurance companies and health maintenance organizations are cutting back on coverage of inpatient chemical dependency treatment. In great part, this is the result of cost-cutting efforts directed at health care in general, but some of the cuts are in response to the twenty-eight day model program. The insurance companies particularly object to the fixed length-of-stay common within inpatient drug treatment programs. A fixed length-of-stay is not common practice in other areas of medicine and psychiatry. Instead, the length-of-stay is determined by the patient's condition. Discharge to outpatient care or some other less restrictive care level is generally determined by specific criteria or treatment progress.

Competition between inpatient programs and the uncertainties of insurance coverage of services have severely stressed many inpatient drug treatment programs. Some programs, however, have responded creatively by developing flexible lengths of stay, day care, and outpatient services.

Chemical Dependency Recovery Hospitals

State health care licensing agencies mandate the staffing patterns of acute care medical and psychiatric hospitals. The regulations prescribe an inappropriately high nurse-to-patient ratios for treatment of most patients who are opiate dependent. The high nurse-to-patient ratio inflates the cost of inpatient treatment without necessarily improving quality of service. To accommodate the staffing needs of inpatient drug abuse treatment, the California Department of Health Services licensed a new class of acute care hospital: the chemical dependency recovery hospital. Many Chemical Dependency Recovery Hospitals (CDRH) are located within a general medical or psychiatric acute care hospital, but a CDRH may also be a free-standing hospital. With a lower nurse-to-patient ratio and services appropriate for chemical dependency treatment, these new hospitals can provide quality inpatient drug abuse treatment at lower costs than that provided in an inpatient hospital licensed as an acute care medical or psychiatric hospital.

Outpatient Treatment

Since there is now an emphasis on shorter lengths of inpatient treatment, use of outpatient services for treatment of opiate dependency has increased. In part, this is made possible by the shorter detoxification time when clonidine instead of methadone is used, and by the availability of naltrexone to prevent early relapse.

NARCOTICS ANONYMOUS

Narcotics Anonymous separated from Alcoholics Anonymous in the 1950s because many opiate addicts felt the need for a separate program to address their opiate dependence. Even though most opiate abusers also abused alcohol, the lifestyle of alcoholics and street opiate addicts differed greatly. AA emphasized abstinence from alcohol; NA emphasized abstinence from all major mood-altering drugs.[2]

Whether to include NA and other self-help recovery groups such as AA among treatment approaches is currently a matter of controversy.[3]

NA does not define participation in NA as drug-abuse treatment, but rather as membership in a recovery fellowship with a spiritual program.[4] The reluctance of NA and other Twelve Step programs to call what they do *treatment* is in part based on practical considerations. By defining themselves as "not treatment," NA and other Twelve Step programs avoid territorial conflicts with practitioners and medical institutions, and they avoid many of the legal liabilities — for example, malpractice — associated with the professional practice. Regardless, most recovery-oriented treatment center staff consider NA and other self-help recovery groups cornerstones of treatment, particularly following inpatient treatment. NA and drug-free recovery treatment share the same primary goal — abstinence from opiates and other drugs of abuse.

Table 1 lists the Twelve Steps of Alcoholics Anonymous, which have been adapted for use by Narcotics Anonymous. The only major change required is substituting "addiction" for "alcohol" in Step One, and substituting "addicts" for "alcoholics" in Step Twelve.

Table 1. The Twelve Steps of Narcotics Anonymous*

1. We admitted that we were powerless over our addiction, that our lives had become unmanageable.
2. We came to believe that a Power greater than ourselves could restore us to sanity.
3. We made a decision to turn our will and our lives over to the care of God *as we understood Him.*
4. We made a searching and fearless moral inventory of ourselves.
5. We admitted to God, to ourselves, and to another human being the exact nature of our wrongs.
6. We were entirely ready to have God remove all these defects of character.
7. We humbly asked Him to remove our shortcomings.
8. We made a list of all persons we had harmed, and became willing to make amends to them all.
9. We made direct amends to such people wherever possible, except when to do so would injure them or others.
10. We continued to take personal inventory and when we were wrong promptly admitted it.
11. We sought through prayer and meditation to improve our conscious contact with God *as we understood Him,* praying only for knowledge of His will for us and the power to carry that out.
12. Having had a spiritual awakening as a result of these steps, we tried to carry this message to addicts, and to practice these principles in all our affairs.

---

* Adapted from the Twelve Steps of Alcoholics Anonymous, and reprinted with permission of AA World Services, Inc., New York, N.Y.

SPIRITUALITY, RELIGION, AND RECOVERY

The incorporation of the concept of Higher Power and God in Steps Two, Three, Five, Six, Seven, and Eleven is a barrier to many people's participation in Twelve Step groups. Clearly, many of the Steps of AA evolved from Christian tradition. Even though the notions of Higher Power and God are liberally defined in practice, the Steps evoke a God or Power that is responsive to prayer.

People who are atheistic, or those who are alienated from or feel persecuted by organized religions, may associate Twelve Step spirituality with religion, and reject participation in needed recovery support. For example, gay I.V. opiate users who perceive themselves as repressed by traditional religion may resist entering what they see as a religious program.

Counselors of opiate-dependent patients need to be aware of these points of resistance to prevent their clients from rejecting a powerful source of recovery support. Counselors should emphasize that spirituality is not synonymous with religion. Religions are comprised of a particular set of beliefs, traditions, and practices, whereas spirituality is the relationship between people and the nonmaterial world. One can be deeply spiritual without practicing any particular religion or belonging to a church. The framework alluded to in Step Three, "God *as we understood Him*" can be broadly interpreted to encompass both religious and spiritual traditions.[5]

With recognition of the power of fellowship, the philosophy embedded in the Twelve Steps, some people have proposed removing the God references in the Twelve Steps. (Such groups exist — for example, the Secular Organization for Sobriety.) As a movement, however, this has not established firm roots.

MANY PATHS TO RECOVERY

Many hospital and community-based drug abuse treatment programs have incorporated Twelve Step work into their treatment regimens. The marriage of self-help recovery movements and chemical dependency treatment usually works to the advantage of treatment, but not always. When particpating in a treatment program that is closely associated with NA and AA, patients who have difficulty with the spiritual nature of NA and AA may also reject the treatment program.

Another problem can arise when the program treatment staff conceptualize the Twelve Step route to recovery as the *only* path to recovery, rather than one of several routes. Treatment plans may not always respond to the needs of the patient, because they reflect this preconceived ideology.[6] This has been a particular problem for "two-hatters": chemical dependency program treatment staff who are themselves recovering from alcoholism or other drug dependencies. They tend to believe that what worked for them will work for their patients. Such counselors may not be able to work effectively with someone who resists the counselor's particular path to recovery.

Recovery-Sensitive Psychotherapists

Enhancing the partnership between Twelve Step recovery programs and psychotherapists is one of the most important tasks in the opiate addiction treatment field. Recovery-oriented psychotherapists often assume a synergy between psychotherapy and Twelve Step programs that will help patients maintain abstinence from opiates.

The recovery-sensitive psychotherapist can also be valuable in redefining the opiate-dependent patient's perception of addiction and in helping to remove the barriers to Twelve Step participation. In addition, these therapists can explain the Twelve Step meeting process and use concrete guidelines, such as the "rule of ten" proposed by Dr. Stan Gitlow,[7] to aid clients in making use of Twelve Step meetings.

1. Attend at least a meeting a day until one or, better, two groups seem to offer more to you than others.
2. Thereafter, never fail to attend these particular meetings.
3. Always arrive before everybody else and with such consistency that your absence would be noteworthy.
4. Always sit in the front row.
5. Introduce yourself to the people seated around you should there be anyone with whom you are not acquainted.
6. Always raise your hand to enter the discussion, no matter how minor your comments.
7. Ask the chairperson to assign a task to you, whether passing the basket, picking up the chairs, or pouring the coffee.
8. Never leave a meeting without sharing a beverage and some discussion with another attendee.
9. Be the last to leave the meeting, and always request someone's company (for a bite to eat and one-on-one dialogue).
10. Whether or not you designate someone as your formal sponsor, choose a successfully abstinent member of the group who attends regularly and meet that person socially between meetings.

Such an approach not only facilitates participation in the recovery process, but also helps the dependent person develop a network of drug-free people who can take the place of their drug-using friends.

Twelve Step recovery programs are traditionally ones of attraction rather than promotion. While this tradition resulted in fewer people being reached, the people who attended Twelve Step meetings generally had a desire to quit using drugs. Today, however, judges, employers, and drug treatment programs mandate documented participation in Twelve Step recovery meetings. The results of involuntary participation are mixed. Some drug abusers who begin attending because they "have to" become motivated to quit using drugs. Others undermine the motivation of voluntary participants.

THERAPEUTIC COMMUNITIES

Therapeutic communities also have historical ties with AA. AA began as a result of its interactions with the Oxford Group[8] movement, which held to four absolutes: absolute honesty, absolute unselfishness, absolute purity, and absolute love. These absolutes predated the Twelve Steps. The Oxford Group also stressed the five Cs: confidence, confession, conviction, conversion, and continuation. The group was deeply involved in Christian values. The movement away from the Oxford Group and emphasis on spirituality resulted in part from an interaction between Bill Wilson, one of the cofounders of AA, and Carl Jung. Jung stressed that the compulsion to use alcohol was so strong that only a spiritual experience was likely to rid the alcoholic of the compulsion.

First Wave Therapeutic Communities

In 1959, Charles Dederick, a recovering alcoholic involved with the fellowship of AA, founded Synanon in Santa Monica, California. He melded his own philosophy, the principles of AA, and the concept of a therapeutic community developed by Maxwell Jones for the treatment of mental illness into a drug-free treatment modality. Initially, opiate addicts were the primary members of Synanon.[9]

Therapeutic communities emphasized personal responsibility, honesty, self-reliance, drug abstinence, self-disclosure, peer support, and the self-help philosophy of AA. The values of the community were reinforced with verbal confrontation and strong discipline.

In keeping with the theory of addiction at that time, Dederick's therapeutic community focused on restructuring the addict's character and environment. The cardinal rule of the therapeutic community was no drugs and no violence.

Second Wave Therapeutic Communities

Second generation therapeutic communities were developed on the East Coast by Synanon alumni. Daytop Lodge in New York was established in 1963 as an experimental program for opiate addicted felons on parole. The second wave of therapeutic communities put its greatest emphasis on criminals who were heroin addicts and were perceived as the most difficult to treat.

Government programs and prisons such as Lexington had a very low success rate, and sociologists such as Lindersmith, in 1947,[10] stressed that although the opiate addict should not be jailed, the only practical approach to opiate dependence was the provision of legal opiates since addicts could not stay drug-free. Therapeutic communites were new hope. Therapeutic communities treated thousands of patients, and challenged the therapeutic pessimism that dominated the criminal justice field and sociology.

On the West Coast, the Mendocino Family in Northern California was a prototype for many therapeutic communities developed within large institutions, such as the Veterans Administration Hospitals and state psychiatric hospitals. The Mendocino Family also stimulated the development of adolescent chemical dependency treatment programs such as Thunder Road, an adolescent treatment program in Oakland, California that is a blend between a therapeutic community and social model residential chemical dependency treatment. Unlike the early therapeutic communities, which shunned outside government support and were supported by donations and resources developed by the people living in the therapeutic communities, these second wave treatment programs were a product of mainstream society and are funded by insurance and public contracts. Walden House in San Francisco, which originated as a traditional therapeutic community, has also evolved in the direction of funded chemical dependency treatment.

Third Wave Therapeutic Communities

There is now a third wave of therapeutic communities.
These programs have broadened their range of clients to include cocaine abusers, crack abusers, polydrug abusers, and prescription drug abusers.[11] Changing drug-abuse patterns, particularly cocaine and crack abuse, and the trend toward multiple drug abuse have resulted in patients with higher degrees of psychological distress. This requires that the modern therapeutic community be more psychiatrically sophisticated to increase the client's awareness of the need to address psychological difficulties and the staff acceptance of psychotropic medication.[12] Psychopathology in those patients often requires medication, such as lithium for manic-depressive disorder, antipsychotic medication for thought disorders such as schizophrenia, or antidepressant medication for endogenous depression.

Chapter 3
ENDNOTES

1. D. Muhleman, "12-Step Study Groups in Drug Abuse Treatment Programs," *Journal of Psychoactive Drugs* 19, no. 3 (1987): 291-98. M. C. Wallen et al., "Utilization of Step Theme Groups in a Short Term Chemical Dependence Treatment Unit," *Journal of Psychoactive Drugs* 19, no. 3 (1987): 287-90.
2. D. E. Smith, H. B. Milkman, and S. G. Sanderwirth, "Addictive Disease, Concept and Controversy," in H. B. Milkman and H. J. Shaeffer, eds., *The Addictions: Multidisciplinary Perspectives and Treatment* (Lexington, Mass.: Lexington Books, 1985), 145-59. H. B. Milkman and S. Sanderwirth, "Addictive Processes," *Journal of Psychoactive Drugs* 17 (1985): 177-92.

3. J. E. Zweben, D. E. Smith, and M. E. Buxton, "Professional Treatment and the Twelve Step Process," *Journal of Psychoactive Drugs*, no. 3 (1987): 227-29. H. W. Clark, "On Professional Therapists and Alcoholics Anonymous," *Journal of Psychoactive Drugs* 19, no. 3 (1987): 275-86.

4. *Narcotics Anonymous,* 3rd ed. (Van Nuys, Calif.: Narcotics Anonymous World Service Office, 1986).

5. M. E. Buxton, D. E. Smith, and R. B. Seymour, "Spirituality and Other Points of Resistance to the 12-Step Recovery Process," *Journal of Psychoactive Drugs* 19, no. 3 (1987): 275-86.

6. Clark, "On Professional Therapists and Alcoholics Anonymous," 233-42.

7. S. Gitlow, "Considerations on the Evelation and Treatment of Substance Dependence," *Journal of Substance Abuse Treatment* 2 (1985): 175-79.

8. The Oxford Group was a nondenominational, theologically conservative evangelical group founded in 1908 by Frank Buchman. It became known as the Oxford Group because of Buchman's preaching among Oxford students during the 1920s and 1930s.

9. L. Yoblonsky, *Synanon: The Tunnel Back* (New York: Macmillan, 1965).

10. A. R. Lindersmith, *Opiate Addiction* (Evanston, Ind.: Principia Press, 1947).

11. S. J. Yohay and C. Winick, "AREBA — Casriel Institute: A Third-Generation Therapeutic Community," *Journal of Psychoactive Drugs* 18, no. 3 (1986): 231-37.

12. N. Jainchill, G. De Leon, and L. Pinkham, "Psychiatric Diagnosis Among Substance Abusers in Therapeutic Community Treatment," *Journal of Psychoactive Drugs* 18, no. 3 (1986): 209-13.

4
DETOXIFICATION

Chronic exposure of brain cells to opiate drugs induces changes resulting in withdrawal symptoms when the opiate use is stopped. The process of change in the brain cells, called *neuroadaptation,* can be illustrated by reference to a particular type of brain cell called the *noradrenergic neurons.* (The cells are called *noradrenergic* because the cells communicate with one another by releasing a neurotransmitter, noradrenalin — also called norepinephrine.)

A diagram of one of the noradrenergic neurons is shown in Figure 1. There are millions of these cells within the brain.

Figure 1. Diagram of a nerve cell

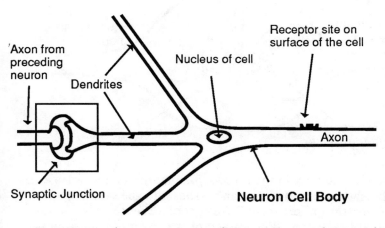

Noradrenergic neurons occur in many areas of the brain, but are particularly concentrated in a small area in the brainstem known as the *locus coeruleus.* The cells form a complicated network of interconnections, with each cell having hundreds or thousands of connecting cells. The cell's firing rate, which controls autonomic functions such as blood pressure, heart rate, and to an extent, anxiety, is influenced by input from connecting cells and receptors on the surface of the cells. Cells are functionally connected to one another by the *synaptic junction,* which is shown within the box in Figure 1.

CELL COMMUNICATION

Figure 2 is an enlargement of the area shown in Figure 1. It illustrates how the cells communicate with one another.

Figure 2. Diagram of the synaptic junction

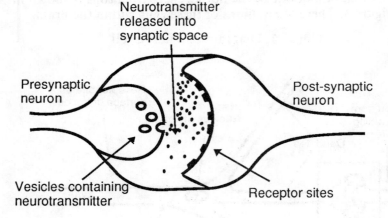

Neurotransmitter
released into
synaptic space

Presynaptic
neuron

Post-synaptic
neuron

Vesicles containing
neurotransmitter

Receptor sites

Electrical activity in the *presynaptic neuron* causes release of specific chemicals from storage vesicles into the synaptic space. The neurotransmitter attaches to specific receptor sites on the postsynaptic neuron. When many of the receptors are occupied by the neurotransmitter, the postsynaptic neuron fires, thus influencing subsequent cells in the chain.

The firing rate is further influenced by receptors located on the *cell body*. Although Figure I shows only one receptor on the surface of the cell, an actual noradrenergic neuron may have hundreds of such receptor sites.

Noradrenergic neurons have at least two types of receptors on the cell body; one is an opiate receptor designated with the Greek letter mu, and the other is a receptor for norepinephrine designated alpha-2.

Morphine, heroin, and other opiates, and some opiate-like compounds produced in the body (enkephalins) attach to the mu-opiate receptor; when the receptor is occupied by an opiate, the firing rate of the neuron is reduced.

When an opiate occupies the mu-opiate receptor most of the time, the cells try to defeat the opiate's effect by increasing their sensitivity. This process is called *neuroadaptation*.

After the neurons adapt to the presence of opiates, they become hyperactive when opiates are removed. This hyperactivity of the noradrenergic neurons cause most of the symptoms that occur during opiate withdrawal.

As previously mentioned, the noradrenergic cells have not only mu-opiate receptors, but another type of receptor called alpha-2, the receptor stimulated by clonidine.

Thus when morphine, heroin, or other opiates stimulate the mu-opiate receptor, the noradrenergic neurons discharge more slowly; when clonidine stimulates the alpha-2 receptor, the neurons also discharge more slowly. Thus, opiates and clonidine have the same effect on the noradrenergic neurons; both reduce the firing rate. This common effect explains why clonidine suppresses opiate withdrawal, even though clonidine does not attach to opiate receptors or have pharmacological properties of opiates. (Opiate-induced euphoria is produced by mu-opiate receptors on other types of neurons that do not have alpha-2 receptors.)

THE RELATIONSHIP OF WITHDRAWAL SYMPTOMS TO NARCOTIC USE

Figure 3 diagrams the addiction cycle driven by physical dependence.

Figure 3. Maintenance of narcotic use by withdrawal symptoms

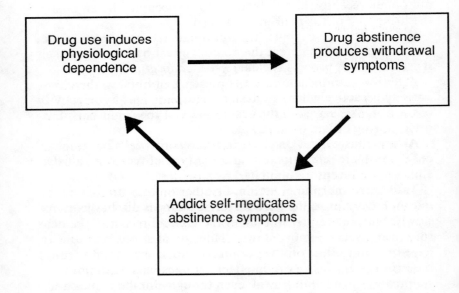

For opiate-dependent individuals, abstinence from opiates produces both *withdrawal symptoms* and a *craving* for narcotics. Table 2 lists physical symptoms of opiate withdrawal.

Table 2. Symptoms of Opiate Withdrawal

Nausea and vomiting
Sweating
Goose flesh
Restlessness
Tremors
Tearing
Runny nose
Yawning
Crampy abdominal pain
Diarrhea
Muscle aches
Feeling cold, shivering
Dilated pupils

Opiate addicts respond by self-medicating these symptoms with additional opiate use. Additional opiate use prolongs or intensifies physical dependence. Thus, the cycle, once begun, is difficult for the addict to interrupt.

Treatment of withdrawal symptoms is one way of exiting the cycle. Unfortunately, the opiate addict may perceive this as the only treatment needed. Rarely, however, is opiate withdrawal itself sufficient treatment. Addiction to opiates is driven by factors in addition to physical dependence. Therefore, withdrawal treatment is mostly important as an opportunity to introduce the patient to treatment of addiction in all its aspects — physical, emotional, and spiritual.

Except in the case of opiate abusers to be maintained on methadone, detoxifying a person who is physically dependent on opiates is an initial treatment step. The goal of detoxification is to provide a safe, comfortable withdrawal from the opiate.

Detoxification services are usually medical treatment model-oriented, but not always — some therapeutic communities have integrated a cold turkey approach to heroin withdrawal into their treatment. Free clinics such as the Haight-Ashbury

Free Medical Clinics in San Francisco help clients withdraw from drugs of abuse as outpatients, using suportive counseling, clonidine, and other non-narcotic medication.

PRINCIPLES OF DETOXIFICATION

A detoxification strategy organized around guiding principles will help to detoxify addicts who use unusual drugs or drug combinations. The following principles apply to detoxifying patients from a variety of opiate and non-opiate drugs.

Principle One: Whenever possible, a long-acting medication is substituted for a short-acting drug of addiction. For example, methadone is substituted for heroin; phenobarbital, a long-acting barbiturate, is substituted for short-acting barbiturates like secobarbital, pentobarbital, amobarbital, or for other short-acting sedative-hypnotics like methaqualone; Valium (diazepam), or Librium (chlordiazepoxide), both long-acting benzodiazepines, are substituted for alcohol. A long-acting medication results in smaller fluctuations of the medication in blood levels between doses, so the withdrawal period is free of the cyclical variations from feeling "high" to withdrawal symptoms.

Principle Two: Intoxication is not necessary to prevent a person from developing withdrawal signs and symptoms. Although patients often request more medication during detoxification, this is often drug-seeking behavior in the absence of actual withdrawal symptoms.

Principle Three: Immediate reduction of 20 to 30 percent of the intoxicating dosage a person has been taking will not produce withdrawal symptoms.

Principle Four: A fixed, divided dose schedule with provisions for omitting dosages if the patient is intoxicated or sleeping has proved to be both the easiest and safest way to accomplish withdrawal. The opiate-dependent have shown they cannot control their dose — drug addicts become drug-dependent because they are unable to control their own use.

Principle Five: Long-term slow withdrawal without the patient's knowledge of the dosage is the generally preferred method of outpatient detoxification. Many patients become anxious when they see their daily dose of medication being reduced. Slow detoxification also allows the treatment team more time to develop continuing care treatment plan.

PHARMACOLOGICAL TREATMENT OF OPIATE WITHDRAWAL

Many medications have been used for opiate detoxification, including methadone, Darvon (propoxyphene HCl), Darvon-N (propoxyphene napsylate), Thorazine (chlorpromazine HCl), and Valium (diazepam). Today, most clinics use either methadone or clonidine for opiate withdrawal.

Methadone

Methadone can be used for withdrawal of heroin, fentanyl, or any other opiate. Except for hospitalized opiate-dependent patients who have a severe medical illness in addition to their opiate dependency, methadone can only be administered for detoxification in a hospital or an outpatient program that is licensed for methadone detoxification. (Opiate-dependent inpatients who are being treated for an acute medical illness can be administered methadone to prevent withdrawal or for detoxification when opiate withdrawal would compromise treatment of their medical condition.)

The withdrawal protocols will vary somewhat depending on where the detoxification is being done.

Inpatient Drug Treatment Program Licensed for Methadone Detoxification

A starting dose of 40 mg per day of methadone is adequate to prevent severe withdrawal symptoms in most opiate-dependent patients. The methadone is administered in doses four times daily, beginning with 10 mg doses. The patient is observed two hours after each dose. If the patient is sleepy, the next dose is decreased to 5 mg. If the patient shows *objective* signs of opiate withdrawal, the following dose is increased to 15 mg. After the first twenty-four hours, the methadone is withdrawn by 5 mg per day. Thus, most patients are withdrawn over eight days.

Outpatient Methadone Detoxification Clinics

In an outpatient clinic, it is usually feasible to administer the doses no more than twice daily. Thus, 20 mg of methadone given twice daily is a good starting point.

Inpatients are generally more tolerant of symptoms than outpatients, and some outpatients may need the starting methadone increased to 60 mg per day to prevent an unacceptable level of opiate withdrawal symptoms. After the second day, the methadone is tapered by 2.5 mg per day. Except as noted below, the methadone withdrawal must be completed within twenty-one days.

Methadone detoxification has traditionally been limited to twenty-one days by federal and state regulations. Dispensing methadone to an opiate abuser for more than twenty-one days was considered methadone maintenance. In 1989, federal regulations were published that allow short-term methadone detoxification of thirty days and long-term detoxification of one hundred and eighty days. Thus, federal programs can implement long-term detoxification in opiate abusers who do not meet requirements for methadone maintenance. As the state methadone licensing agencies develop regulations parallel to the federal regulations, methadone programs that are licensed by the state can also implement long-term methadone detoxification.[1]

Clonidine

In 1978, the publication of Gold, et al. in *Lancet,* called attention to clonidine's effectiveness in suppressing symptoms of opiate withdrawal. [2] Since then, addiction specialists have commonly used oral clonidine for this purpose, even though it is not approved by the Food and Drug Administration for treatment of opiate withdrawal.

Clonidine also has some advantages over methadone for treating narcotic withdrawal.[3]

1. Clonidine is not a scheduled drug that is subject to abuse.
2. The use of opiates can be discontinued immediately in preparation for naltrexone induction or admission to drug-free treatments such as a therapeutic community.
3. The absence of euphoria from clonidine reduces drug-seeking behavior.

Clonidine Transdermal Patch

In 1986, a transdermal patch containing clonidine was approved for use in the United States. Although the clonidine patch is marketed for the treatment of hypertension, addiction specialists quickly grasped the potential of the patch for the treatment of opiate withdrawal.

The clonidine patch (Catapress-TTS) is a 0.2 mm-thick, self-adhesive, square patch that looks and applies like a Band-Aid. The patch is formed of four layers and is available in three sizes: 3.5, 7.0, and 10.5 cm sq. In a twenty-four hour period each patch delivers an amount of clonidine equivalent to twice daily dosing with 0.1, 0.2, or 0.3 mg oral clonidine, respectively. Once placed on the epidermal surface, clonidine enters the circulation system through the skin. A rate-limiting membrane within the patch governs the maximum amount absorbed. Although the manufacturer recommends replacement of the patch after seven days, pharmacokinetic studies have shown that the patch delivers clonidine for up to twelve days.

Thus, in treatment of opiate withdrawal, one application of the patch is sufficient.

In a recovery-oriented inpatient drug treatment program such as Merritt Peralta Institute in Oakland where use of the patch was first reported, the transdermal patches offer certain advantages over oral clonidine:[4]

1. Minimizes drug-seeking behavior on the ward.
2. Eliminates dosage administration disruptions of patient's program activities.
3. Prevents build-up of withdrawal symptoms during the night.

Minimizes Drug-Seeking Behavior

Recovery-oriented chemical dependency units have a different milieu than medical units. The treatment personnel are alert to drug-seeking behavior and, unless the patient is demonstrating objective signs of withdrawal, staff may view requests for medication as drug-seeking behavior. Nurses in such treatment units usually try to minimize such behavior, and they often question the patient's need for medication unless objective opiate withdrawal symptoms are present.

Eliminates Disruptions

Because oral clonidine must be administered several times each day, chemical dependency counselors often complain about disruption to groups or counseling sessions when patients need to leave to receive their "pills."

Asymptomatic patients may forget to go to the nurses' station at scheduled times, miss doses when they are attending outside activities, or be pressured by other patients or counselors not to leave meetings. Some patients whose clonidine level dropped due to missed dosing developed opiate withdrawal symptoms.

Prevents Build-Up of Withdrawal Symptoms During the Night

If patients miss doses of oral clonidine during the night because the nurses are reluctant to wake them, they sometimes awaken experiencing opiate withdrawal. Since the clonidine patch continues to deliver clonidine throughout the night, both staff and most patients generally prefer the clonidine patch over oral clonidine. Although not established by controlled study, patients treated with oral clonidine appear to have more withdrawal symptoms than those treated with transdermal clonidine patches.

Using Clonidine for Treatment of Opiate Withdrawal.

Recommended schedules for use of oral clonidine in opiate withdrawal vary widely. Gold et al. recommend 1.2 mg per day in three divided doses;[5] Washton, Resnick, and Rawson recommend 0.2 mg four times a day.[6]

We recommend a *combination* of oral clonidine and the patch, using the following guidelines:

- To patients who are showing objective signs of opiate withdrawal at the initiation of treatment, we administer a 0.2 mg dose of oral clonidine sublingually and apply two or three #2 clonidine transdermal patches: two patches if the patient weighs less than 150 pounds; three patches if the patient weighs more than 150 pounds.
- The 0.2 mg sublingual dose is repeated in one hour if the patient still shows signs of opiate withdrawal.
- After acute opiate withdrawal symptoms subside, we orally administer 0.2 mg of clonidine every six hours for the first two days.

During the first two days, oral doses of clonidine are necessary because it takes time for the patch to begin delivering effective blood levels of clonidine.[7]

For opiate-dependent patients who are not in withdrawal at the time of initial examination, we omit the sublingual dosages, apply the clonidine patches, and administer the oral doses of clonidine.

The patch is left on for seven days for heroin withdrawal and ten days for methadone withdrawal. If the patient has pain during withdrawal, we administer regular therapeutic doses of a non-opiate painkiller, such as aspirin, acetaminophen (for example, Tylenol) or ibuprofen (for example, Motrin).

Side Effects of Clonidine

During clonidine treatment, some patients become dizzy, or feel they are about to faint when they rise from bed quickly. Patients should be told about this possibility and advised to sit on the bed for a couple of minutes before standing up. Clonidine may also produce dry mouth, fatigue, and lethargy.

MIXED OPIATE/SEDATIVE-HYPNOTIC DEPENDENCE

Addicts may abuse both sedative-hypnotics and heroin concurrently, and in sufficient amounts to develop physical dependence on both. Furthermore, some methadone-maintained patients may develop sedative-hypnotic dependence. Either of these cases bring about a complicated detoxification situation.

Mixed Opiate and Sedative-Hypnotic Withdrawal

Unlike opiate withdrawal, sedative-hypnotic withdrawal may result in grand mal seizures, psychosis, and even death. Because the life-threatening sequelae of sedative withdrawal may not be the result of noradrenergic hyperactivity, clonidine may not prevent its occurrence. Clonidine may, however, mask the signs and symptoms of noradrenergic hyperactivity that precede severe withdrawal.[8] Therefore, if clonidine is to be used for opiate withdrawal, the physician must be certain that the replacement of the sedative is adequate to prevent sedative-hypnotic withdrawal symptoms.

If methadone is available for treating opiate withdrawal, a patient who is physically dependent on *both* a sedative-hypnotic (including alcohol) and opiates should be withdrawn from the sedative hypnotic first. During the sedative-hypnotic withdrawal period, the patient is maintained on methadone to prevent opiate withdrawal. After withdrawal of the sedative is complete, the methadone can be withdrawn at 5 mg per day. Protocols for sedative-hypnotic withdrawal are beyond the scope of this book; however, they are available elsewhere.[9]

Using Methadone for Treatment of Opiate Withdrawal

Although methadone is FDA-approved for treatment of opiate withdrawal, it is a potent opiate and is subject to all the controls of other Schedule II medications, plus additional federal and state regulations governing dispensing of methadone for treatment of opiate addiction. Although physicians can prescribe methadone for treatment of pain, physicians are prohibited from treating opiate addiction with methadone except in a specially licensed clinic or hospital.

To treat heroin withdrawal with methadone in a hospital, we generally begin with 10 mg of methadone orally four times a day. If the patient is sleeping soundly at the time a dosage is due, we omit the dose. After two days, we begin to withdraw the methadone at the rate of 5 mg per day. Although 40 mg of methadone daily may be more than that needed to suppress withdrawal symptoms in lightly addicted patients, or may be too little to meet the needs of heavily addicted patients, we have nevertheless found a fixed dosage easier to manage. Titrating a patient's withdrawal symptoms with methadone is needlessly complicated and sets up many opportunities for "stingy parent versus demanding child" interactions between staff and addict.

Darvon-N (Propoxyphene Napsylate)

The use of Darvon-N (propoxyphene napsylate) as a withdrawal agent has generated considerable controversy. Darvon is cross-tolerant with the opiates. The previously low level of statutory controls on Darvon allowed its use in situations for opiate withdrawal, but Darvon is now a Schedule IV narcotic. Legal difficulties arose when the FDA strengthened the role of package inserts and declared that the use of a drug for indications other than those described in the package insert is considered investigational. Because Darvon-N is not approved by the FDA as a treatment for opiate dependence and because it is a Schedule IV narcotic, it should not be used for opiate withdrawal.

Darvon (Propoxyphene Hydrochloride) Dependence

Darvon (propoxyphene HCl) is commonly prescribed, and occasional cases of primary propoxyphene dependence occur. The hydrochloride can be abused intravenously, but the napsylate (Darvon-N) is highly insoluble and cannot be injected.

The propoxyphene withdrawal syndrome is similar to low-dosage opiate withdrawal and can be treated with clonidine.

Talwin (Pentazocine) Dependence

Cases of primary pentazocine dependence occasionally occur, but given the widespread medical use of this compound, the addiction rate is probably low. Withdrawal from pentazocine does not produce the dramatic withdrawal syndrome of opiates or sedative-hypnotics, although acute withdrawal from higher dosages of pentazocine is unpleasant. A suitable longer-acting agent is not available for substitution withdrawal. Clonidine is the preferred withdrawal treatment.

Chapter 4
ENDNOTES

1. "Methadone: Rule, Proposed Rules and Notice," *Federal Register* 54, no. 40 (2 March 1989): 8960.
2. M. W. Gold, D. E. Redmond, and H. D. Kleber, "Clonidine Blocks Acute Opiate Withdrawal Symptoms," - *Lancet* 2, no. 8090 (1978): 599-602.
3. H. W. Clark, and N. Longmuir, "Clonidine Transdermal Patches: A Recovery Oriented Treatment of Opiate Withdrawal," *California Society for the Treatment of Alcoholism and Other Drug Dependencies NEWS* 13 (1986): 1-2.
4. Ibid.
5. M. S. Gold et al., "Opiate Withdrawal Using Clonidine. A Safe, Effective, and Rapid Non-Opiate Treatment," *Journal of the American Medical Association* 243, no. 4 (1980): 343-46.
6. A. M. Washton, R. B. Resnick, and R. A. Rawson, "Clonidine for Outpatient Opiate Intoxication," *Lancet* 1, no. 8177 (1980): 1078-79.
7. T. R. MacGregor et al., "Pharmacokinetics of Transdermally Delivered Clonidine," *Clinical Pharmacology and Therapeutics* 38, no. 3 (1985): 278-84.
8. P. L. Hughes and R. M. Morse, "Use of Clonidine in a Mixed-Drug Detoxification Regimen: Possibility of Masking of Clinical Signs of Sedative Withdrawal," *Mayo Clinic Proceedings* 60, no. 1 (1985): 47-49.
9. D. E. Smith and D. R. Wesson, "Phenobarbital Techniques for Treatment of Barbiturate Dependence," *Archives of Psychiatry* 24, no. 1 (1971): 56-60.

5
METHADONE MAINTENANCE

Although methadone maintenance has been used for treatment of opiate dependence since 1965, serious debate continues among professionals in the United States about the effectiveness, appropriateness, and acceptability of methadone maintenance.[1] In spite of this controversy, methadone maintenance remains an important treatment modality for heroin addiction for three main reasons:

- It is the only treatment many heroin addicts will accept.
- Patient retention in treatment is high.
- Most patients on methadone maintenance reduce their drug abuse and criminal activities.

This chapter reviews current ideas about methadone maintenance, and describes its clinical use and relationship to other forms of drug abuse treatment.

ORIGINS OF METHADONE AS A TREATMENT MODALITY

In the early 1960s, Drs. Vincent Dole and the late Marie Nyswander were conducting studies of morphine metabolism when morphine was given repeatedly. Their research subjects were heroin addicts who had been hospitalized for the research. To withdraw the subjects, Dole and Nyswander selected methadone. Dole and Nyswander repeatedly dosed addicts with morphine; this produced physical dependence in the subjects. To their surprise, the researchers observed that the dysfunction present in many subjects, while they were taking morphine, markedly improved after the subjects were switched to methadone. This observation caused the researchers to propose methadone substitution as a treatment modality. Thus, before the discovery of narcotic receptors, endorphins, or enkephalins, Dole and Nyswander proposed the idea that opiate dependency was a metabolic abnormality. Addicts were either born with some metabolic abnormality that methadone corrected, or that repeated exposure to narcotic drugs induced metabolic changes in neurons.[2]

Dole and Nyswander conducted the first clinical study of methadone maintenance in treatment of heroin addicts. Intravenous opiate addicts who had a history of repeated relapses following withdrawal treatment were hospitalized and given increasing doses of methadone. After subjects reached a dose of methadone of 80 to 120 mg per day, they were discharged from the hospital and continued on methadone maintenance as outpatients. In this study, more than 90 percent of the subjects remained in outpatient methadone maintenance treatment and about 75 percent became, according to Dole and Nyswander, "socially productive and living as normal citizens in the community after only six months of treatment."[3]

From the reduction in symptoms and improvement in behavior, Dole and Nyswander concluded that an addict's psychopathology was a "consequence, not a cause" of addiction. Because methadone maintenance worked better than psychological treatment, they further concluded that opiate addiction probably had a metabolic component, and they used the success of opiate maintenance to support their hypothesis.

MODELS OF METHADONE MAINTENANCE TREATMENT

Programs using methadone differ widely in dosage schedules, take-out policies, ancillary services, treatment philosophy, and goals. Some criticisms of methadone maintenance as a treatment modality stem from unacknowledged differences in treatment goals between advocates of drug-free recovery-oriented treatments and advocates of methadone maintenance.

Advocates of drug-free recovery-oriented treatment believe that methadone maintenance is not a treatment for opiate dependence, since the patient remains opiate-dependent for the duration of treatment. They cite the high frequency with which methadone-maintained patients abuse other drugs — particularly cocaine, alcohol, and marijuana — and the high frequency of relapse when methadone is stopped.

Methadone maintenance proponents emphasize the social benefits of maintenance. Many studies of methadone maintenance show that methadone-maintained patients commit fewer property crimes, decrease illicit opiate use, and decrease needle use. The decrease in needle use is particularly important because of AIDS. By reducing needle sharing, methadone maintenance treatment can decrease the spread of HIV virus.

Cocaine abuse among methadone-maintained patients, however, has to a great extent, undermined the community benefit argument for methadone maintenance. The methadone-maintained patient who regularly abuses cocaine often commits property crimes to acquire cocaine. In addition, high-dose cocaine abuse produces much socially disruptive behavior — paranoid psychosis, violence, and overdose — which often results in medical or psychiatric hospitalization.

Even advocates for methadone maintenance disagree about its role. There are two models of methadone maintenance: (1) *the biochemical abnormality model,* and (2) *the rehabilitative model.* Each model has different goals.

Biochemical Abnormality Model

This model, sometimes called *the adaptive model,* assumes that the opiate addict has a persistent derangement of opiate receptor and endogenous opiate production, and that methadone in adequate doses can compensate.[4] Some believe that the opiate addict is born with the abnormality; others believe that chronic heroin abuse *induces* the abnormality. Regardless of the cause, methadone maintenance is replacement therapy, comparable to giving a diabetic insulin. Failure of methadone to stabilize patients may be due to inadequate blood levels of methadone.* The primary goal of treatment is to improve health and economic and social functioning.

The Rehabilitation Model

In this model, (also called *the change-oriented model),* methadone keeps addicts in treatment and reduces their incentive for opiate use. With the patient's lifestyle changed for the better — at least temporarily — staff can help them acquire the vocational and coping skills necessary for living outside the drug culture. Methadone maintenance is viewed as a pragmatic first step toward achieving a drug-free life. After one to two years of methadone maintenance, the treatment staff expect the patient to discontinue methadone. State and federal regulations about methadone maintenance generally reflect acceptance of this model, and some public funding agencies, faced with waiting lists for methadone maintenance, use it to justify limits on the duration patients can receive treatment in publicly funded methadone maintenance programs.[5]

SCREENING PATIENTS FOR METHADONE MAINTENANCE

Much of the subsequent information in this chapter is based on the methadone maintenance program at the San Francisco Veterans Administration's Substance Abuse Treatment Clinic, where methadone maintenance, naltrexone, and drug-free recovery-oriented treatment are all used to treat opiate dependence.

Many opiate abusers request methadone maintenance when

---

* The optimal pharmacologically effective range of methadone in blood is 150-600 ng/ml (Dole, 1988).

they first seek treatment for opiate dependence. Most come for treatment during a situational crisis and they expect to start methadone maintenance immediately. For both clinical and practical reasons, beginning methadone maintenance immediately is ill-advised. First, the patient must be assessed to determine whether methadone maintenance is clinically indicated. Second, the addict's opiate abuse must be *documented* to determine whether the patient meets state and FDA admission criteria for methadone maintenance.[6]

The structure of the initial contact between the opiate addict and treatment staff is important in determining whether the addict can be engaged in drug abuse treatment. Because most opiate addicts have difficulty dealing with bureaucracies and authority, we try, during the first contact, to establish a positive rapport between staff and patient. We also have to reinforce the patient's motivation for treatment. Patients are given as much information as possible, including an explanation of methadone maintenance programs and admission requirements, as well as information about alternatives to methadone maintenance.

A urine sample is taken and used to document current use and to verify drug abuse history. Patients sign a release-of-information form to allow staff to obtain medical and psychiatric records on previous drug abuse treatment. These records will be used to document length of addiction, to alert the program staff to underlying psychiatric difficulties or propensity for violent behavior, and to give an independent view of the patient's past response to treatment. These and other procedures take place during the initial contact to speed the evaluation process and to comply with FDA regulations.

Clinical Criteria for Admission to Methadone Maintenance

There is no consensus among addiction specialists about clinical criteria for admission to methadone maintenance. Many believe methadone maintenance should be readily available for any opiate abuser who wants it and meets federal admission criteria. Other addiction specialists believe methadone maintenance should be a treatment of last resort, to be instituted only after repeated failures of drug-free treatments.

Most opiate addicts come to the clinic requesting methadone maintenance. That they prefer and meet regulatory requirements for methadone maintenance are important considerations, but not the only ones used in deciding whether methadone maintenance is appropriate. We also require:

1. The patient has a regular place to live.
2. The patient has a compelling reason, such as a job, that precludes treatment in a long-term therapeutic community.
3. The patient must agree to come to the clinic daily for dosing.
4. The patient not be physically dependent on sedative-hypnotics or alcohol.

We attach considerable weight to the patient's progress during previous methadone maintenance treatment. Significant periods of abstinence from abuse of drugs, stable employment, and an orderly, voluntary termination of previous methadone maintenance treatment argue for restarting methadone maintenance. Involuntary termination of previous methadone maintenance treatment because of violence, continued abuse of drugs (particularly cocaine or amphetamines), or failure to participate in treatment would argue against methadone maintenance.

Patients who are not physically dependent on opiates would be encouraged to consider naltrexone.

FEDERAL CRITERIA

FDA regulations, which were revised in 1989, describe the requirements for treatment with methadone maintenance.[7] A patient must prove opiate addiction of more than one year, and addiction for most of the year before entering treatment, generally interpreted as six months and one day in the last twelve months.

The FDA recognizes some exceptions to the requirement for current addiction to opiates.

1. Opiate addicts who have a documented history of addiction and who have just been released from a penal institution or chronic care facility, and who are in imminent danger of relapse to opiate abuse.
2. A pregnant opiate addict.
3. Previous methadone maintenance patients who are reapplying for methadone maintenance within two years following a voluntary discharge from a methadone maintenance clinic and who are clinically assessed to be at risk for relapse.

Adolescent opiate abusers (sixteen to eighteen years of age) must meet more specific requirements: They are required to have had two documented attempts of short-term detoxification or drug-free treatment; a parent, legal guardian, or responsible adult must sign the "Consent to Methadone Treatment" form.

STATE CRITERIA

State requirements for methadone maintenance are usually more restrictive than federal requirements. For example, until 1987, the statutory requirements of the California Department of Alcohol and Drug Abuse required a two-year history of documented opiate addiction and at least two failed treatment attempts before an opiate addict was eligible for methadone maintenance. The requirement for failed treatment attempts was removed because of the relationship between I.V. drug abuse and AIDS.

DOCUMENTING LENGTH OF ADDICTION

The length of addiction can be verified by prior treatment in detoxification clinics, by physicians, and by previous drug treatment programs. Additional documents that may be used include "rap sheets" (arrest records) from the criminal justice system or reports from parole or probation officers. If documentation from treatment programs is unavailable, a notarized letter from the patient's parent or a spouse may be acceptable.

A release-of-information form signed by the patient is usually needed both to obtain records from other treatment programs, and to contact law enforcement agencies, physicians, and hospitals where the patient was previously treated for physical symptoms of withdrawal.

To document *current opiate use,* we collect a urine sample at the initial interview and again five days later.

Documentation of Current Physical Dependence

Once the decision for outpatient induction on methadone maintenance is made, the patient is instructed to return to the clinic in opiate withdrawal. Patients are *clearly* told that they *must* be in opiate withdrawal in order to begin methadone. If the patient does not show objective signs of withdrawal, a naloxone (Narcan) challenge is conducted.* Using a narcotic withdrawal checklist, The Objective Opiate Withdrawal Scale,[8] a physician documents withdrawal symptoms and administers to the patient the first methadone dose.

---

* 0.2 mg of naloxone is injected intravenously. If the patient is opiate dependent, signs and symptoms of opiate withdrawal will develop in one to two minutes.

INITIAL METHADONE DOSING

FDA regulations specify that the first dose of methadone can be no more than 30 mg. Following the first dose, the patient remains in the clinic for two hours. If withdrawal symptoms continue, the patient is given an additional 10 mg of methadone.

For most patients, 30 to 40 mg of methadone will suppress acute heroin withdrawal. The dosage for maintenance can vary widely. People differ in the rate they metabolize methadone, and some patients may require more than standard dosing.[9] Some patients, however, develop withdrawal symptoms before their methadone dose the following day. If withdrawal symptoms develop, the daily methadone dose is increased 10 mg daily until withdrawal symptoms disappear.

TREATMENT PHASES

The treatment of an opiate addict using methadone has four phases:

1. Assessment and stabilization.
2. Achieving abstinence.
3. Maintaining abstinence.
4. Stable abstinence.

First Phase: Assessment and Stabilization

The first phase of treatment has two objectives. The first includes assessing the patient's drug abuse history, completing a medical and psychological evaluation, and evaluating the patient's family members and social support network, current legal problems, and work history and potential. The second is stabilization on methadone.

Heroin use carries the addict through predictable cycles of feeling high, then normal, and finally sick from opiate withdrawal. For most heroin addicts, the cycle occurs several times a day. Their physical, emotional, and mental energies and behavior are dominated by the powerful need for another "fix" to self-medicate withdrawal symptoms. Because it is much longer-acting than heroin, methadone stretches this cycle out to twenty-four hours or longer, and eliminates the daily onsets of withdrawal symptoms. The methadone dosages patients receive are carefully calculated to prevent withdrawal symptoms and stabilize mood.

The daily maintenance dose of methadone ranges from 30 to 80 mg. For most patients, 50 mg is adequate, though a few require 70 to 80 mg to stabilize. In one controlled study, 80 mg per day was more effective than 40 mg.[10] If the patient continues to use heroin while on methadone maintenance, the daily dose of methadone is increased. The goal is to induce sufficient tolerance so reasonable quantities of heroin will not produce euphoria. The maximum daily dose routinely allowed by FDA regulations is 100 mg. Authorization for higher doses can be obtained by notifying the FDA on a case-by-case basis.

In addition to assessment and stabilization on methadone, a treatment plan that will guide psychosocial treatment during the first three months is developed.

After the patient's condition has sufficiently stabilized and narcotic and other substance abuse has ceased, he or she is referred for specialized services such as vocational assessment, family evaluations, or couples counseling. These treatment services can help the patient move naturally into the second phase of treatment, achieving abstinence. If, however, a patient is not abstinent from illicit drugs after six months in treatment, more intensive behavioral interventions take place. At a minimum, patients are expected to have three consecutive months of drug-free urine tests by the end of the first year in treatment. FDA regulations allow patients to self-administer methadone at home three times per week after they have been free of illicit drugs for three months and are employed full-time.

Second Phase: Achieving Abstinence

The second phase objectives are abstinence from all self-administered drugs except methadone and recognition that a change in lifestyle is necessary for recovery. In addition, treatment emphasis changes somewhat from the first phase.

At this time in treatment, many patients continue to episodically use nonopiate drugs, particularly marijuana, cocaine, and alcohol. Consequently, treatment now focuses on helping patients understand the need for abstinence from all drugs — except medications prescribed by a physician for treatment of a disorder other than opiate dependence. They begin learning methods to achieve abstinence.

Patients attend the "abstinence group" that meets twice a week. The primary focus of the group is achieving abstinence from all abused drugs. For example, patients identify triggers for cravings. The group leader and other members of the group suggest ways of avoiding triggers and coping with cravings.

In addition, patients are encouraged to participate regularly in Narcotics Anonymous or other Twelve Step programs. Members of the group may attend Twelve Step meetings together, and they might meet for activities outside the group.

Patients are further encouraged to continue any uncompleted medical treatments, to make appointments for psychotherapy or other forms of mental health treatment that have been recommended, and to work toward resolution of legal problems. Staff now helps patients focus more on developing positive family and social support systems.

Prior to entering treatment, patients spent their time in drug-related pursuits: finding money for drugs, acquiring drugs, and using drugs. Now they must begin developing activities that will maintain sobriety — not an easy task. Detailed vocational or leisure time assessments in conjunction with good counseling can help. Some patients will enter school or other educational activities.

Third Phase: Maintaining Abstinence (Early Recovery and Prevention of Relapse)

During the third phase of treatment — a critical time for the patient — additional techniques of relapse prevention are brought into play. As the acute legal, family, or medical problems that initiated treatment are resolved, the patient may feel "cured" and able to resume nonopiate drug use. The notion of *cure* is discouraged at every opportunity.

Once the patient has achieved three months of abstinence and has attended thirty-six self-help meetings, he or she graduates to a recovery support group. The focus of this group is maintaining abstinence. A primary task is time restructuring (for example, vocational rehabilitation, enrollment in school, and use of leisure time).

The focus of the recovery support group process is coping with feelings. Patients often describe dysphoric feelings such as remorse, guilt, sadness, and grief — related to past abuses of relationships, and "giving up" the pursuit and use of drugs that the recovering addict now remembers as exciting, pleasurable, or both. In addition, the addict's shift in lifestyle often produces interpersonal estrangement from friends or lovers who are still using. The addict does not tolerate the emergence of these powerful feelings — which may be perceived as alien, threatening, and overwhelming. The feelings become major risks for relapse because an addict's usual response to strong feelings is to alter them with drugs. The buffering of the feelings by the prescribed methadone can be of therapeutic assistance by reducing overwhelming feelings to tolerable levels.

The group leader's task is to support the patient's handling of feelings. The group process is useful in many ways. By finding out, for example, that others have similar feelings, the patient's sense of isolation and uniqueness is reduced. The addict, who is not used to discussing feelings, may believe that he or she is the only one who has such "abnormal" feelings. By telling how they have successfully dealt with similar feelings, other group members can support the patient to develop new coping methods. The group leader, by relabeling the feelings as "normal" human emotions, can also be supportive.

The program can also support the patient. Most patients view "take home" methadone as a special privilege or reward.

Self-help meetings continue to be important in reinforcing sobriety and preventing the patient's abuse of nonopiate drugs. Medical and psychiatric conditions are monitored with an additional emphasis on health maintenance.

About 50 percent of our patients are either employed or are full-time students during this phase. The other half are either chronically disabled for medical or psychiatric reasons or marginally functioning but without legal disability. This latter 50 percent have major difficulty in developing appropriate daily activities. In many ways, involvement in activities is easier for the chronically disabled group, who are eligible for social services in the community, than it is for the marginally functioning group.

A recent innovation in methadone maintenance is a closer tie with Narcotic Anonymous. NA groups vary in their receptivity to patients on methadone maintenance. In some NA groups, methadone-maintained patients are not welcome; in others, they are. We believe the Twelve Steps are important to reinforce the ideas of drug abstinence and the concept that recovery from substance abuse is a lifelong process.

Fourth Phase: Stable Abstinence

After patients have been on methadone maintenance for two years, are employed full-time, and are abstinent from all illicit drug use for at least six months, they are required to come to the clinic only twice a week. All patients are urged to continue meeting with their counselor, attend Twelve Step meetings, and, in some cases, group psychotherapy. Some patients, however, abstain from abuse of opiates and other drugs, yet resist participating in clinic or Twelve Step meetings. Such patients often have no desire to stop methadone, and they relapse when they are forced to stop. Both the community and the patient are best served by the patient's continued methadone maintenance. The patient continues urine monitoring; the patient meets with his or her counselor monthly, and his or her treatment plan is reviewed every six months as required by the FDA.

FAILURE TO PROGRESS IN TREATMENT

If the patient shows no significant progress after six months of treatment, the patient's counselor, in consultation with the rest of the patient's treatment team, develops a behavioral contingency contract. The contract will sometimes help patients become abstinent when other approaches are failing. If the patient has not broken any of the administrative program rules, a counselor meets with the patient and discusses the lack of treatment progress and the need for a change in the treatment. Failure to comply with the contingency contract results in the loss of clinic privileges or suspension. If the issue is continued drug use, the contract may provide that the patient's methadone dose will be decreased 5 to10 mg for each subsequent drug-positive urine. (If the methadone dose is reduced to 20 mg, the patient will be tapered off methadone over a twenty-one day period.) The contract will generally specify conditions for reinstatement of his or her usual dose of methadone or take-out privileges. For example, the dose may be restored by submitting three weekly drug-free urine tests in a row.

Many clinics struggle with the issue of whether to suspend patients who are not progressing in their treatment programs. Although substance abuse is a chronic relapsing disorder, and relapses can be expected, patients nevertheless have a responsibility to work actively toward abstinence. Some patients need a hiatus from treatment when they are not interested in working on their problem.

As a rule-of-thumb, patients who fail to progress in treatment during the first treatment attempt are usually suspended for three months. If they fail in the second episode of treatment, with stricter supervisory controls, they may be suspended for six months. After third and subsequent failures in treatment, we strongly recommend either residential treatment or some other non-outpatient program. We are, however, lenient in reaccepting patients, and will usually reconsider applications for readmission after one year.

These procedures help maintain the program's integrity, support the staff, and increase the patients' awareness of the consequences of their behaviors and their addiction.

Methadone maintenance has a role in the continuum of outpatient treatment services for long-term, heroin-dependent people who need to, or insist on, remaining in the community.

Chapter 5
ENDNOTES

1. T. F. Kirn, "Methadone Maintenance Treatment Remains Controversial Even after 23 Years of Experience," *Journal of the American Medical Association* 260, no. 20 (1988): 2970.
2. V. P. Dole and M. E. Nyswander, "Heroin Addiction: A Metabolic Disease," *Archives of Internal Medicine* 120, no. 1 (1967): 19-24.
3. Ibid.
4. V. P. Dole, "Implications of Methadone Maintenance for Theories of Narcotic Addiction," *Journal of the American Medical Association* 260, no. 20 (1988): 3025-29.
5. M. Rosenbaum, S. Murphy, and J. Beck, "Money for Methadone: Preliminary Findings from a Study of Alameda County's Maintenance Policy," *Journal of Psychoactive Drugs* 19, no. 1 (1987): 13-19.
6. Treatment provided on a federal enclave, such as a

military base or Veterans Administration medical center, may be exempt from state restrictions.

7. "Methadone; Rule, Proposed Rules, and Notice," *Federal Register* 54, no. 40 (2 March 1989): 8954-79.
8. L. Handelsman et al., "Two New Rating Scales for Opiate Withdrawal," *American Journal of Drug and Alcohol Abuse* 13, no. 3 (1987): 297.
9. F. S. Tennant, Jr., "Inadequate Plasma Methadone Concentrations in Some High-Dose Methadone Patients," *American Journal of Psychiatry* 144 (1987): 1349-50.
10. A. Goldstein and B. A. Judson, "Efficacy and Side Effects of Three Widely Different Methadone Doses, *Proceedings 5th National Conference on Methadone Treatment* (New York: National Association for the Prevention of Addiction to Narcotics 1973).

6
NALTREXONE

Naltrexone, marketed by DuPont Pharmaceuticals under the trade name Trexan, was approved by the FDA for use in treatment of opiate dependency in 1984. Naltrexone blocks the effects of opiates by attaching itself to the mu-opiate receptor — the receptor through which opiates produce mood-altering and painkilling effects. Naltreone prevents an opiate molecule's access to the receptor. This is illustrated in Figure 4.

Figure 4. Naltrexone binds to the opiate receptor site and prevents the opiate molecule's access to it.

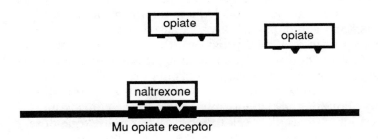

Naltrexone has no other effect of its own at the opiate receptor. Some molecules of naltrexone remain on the receptor even after blood levels are very low. The half-life of blockage at the receptor ranged from seventy-two to one hundred eight hours[1] which far exceeds the half-life of naltrexone in blood (four to twelve hours) or the metabolite of naltrexone, beta-naltrexol. Clinical observations show that 50 mg per day of oral naltrexone will block the effects of heroin for twenty-four hours or more.

Since naltrexone has no opiate effects of its own, but instead prevents a narcotic from exerting its effects, naltrexone is called a *narcotic antagonist*. The pharmacological effectiveness of naltrexone is unquestioned. Nevertheless, its overall role in preventing relapse is less certain.

COMPLIANCE WITH NALTREXONE TREATMENT

The biggest difficulty with naltrexone as a treatment modality is getting recovering opiate-dependent individuals to take it. Given their choice of naltrexone or methadone, most heroin addicts will choose the latter. Unlike methadone and other opiate agonists, naltrexone does not produce pleasant mood effects, nor does it cause withdrawal symptoms after a missed dose. Retention of opiate addicts on naltrexone is generally shorter than on methadone. The poor retention is attributed to poor motivation, inadequate treatment models, side effects,[2] and addict personality characteristics.

Within drug treatment programs, the models of naltrexone treatment are derived from methadone. Following the methadone use treatment pattern, patients are generally administered their naltrexone dose in the clinic. Self-administration is rarely allowed, and patients must come to the clinic from three to five times per week to receive their naltrexone dose. Although former heroin abusers are often willing to come to a clinic and stand in line to receive methadone, they are less willing to do so for naltrexone. Most opiate abusers find the mood-altering effects of methadone desirable. They do not obtain such effects from naltrexone. Further, since the therapeutic effects of naltrexone prevent opportunistic relapse, patients' motivation to take naltrexone is primarily influenced by their perception of relapse risk and their motivation for abstinence. Finally, most people, not only opiate abusers, have difficulty complying for even a short time with a medication regimen designed to prevent, rather than cure, an illness.

For patients who are motivated to abstain from opiate use, naltrexone can be a valuable recovery tool. Its use ensures that euphoria and other mood effects from narcotics will not occur during the twenty-four to seventy-two hours after naltrexone is taken. Narcotic cravings are generally reduced, and impulsive use of heroin less likely.

Furthermore, naltrexone allows the patients time for problem resolution and growth by helping free them from the physiologically driven preoccupation with opiate cravings and use.

Naltrexone is uniquely appropriate and useful for physicians, nurses, veterinarians, pharmacists, and dentists who are recovering from narcotic dependency. Because it has no narcotic effect, naltrexone is compatible with drug-free philosophy. In addition, naltrexone is the only narcotic-dependency medication acceptable to most licensing boards. By monitoring naltrexone ingestion, the licensing board or hospital staff can be assured that the recovering health professional is not under the influence of an opiate while at work.

We conducted an efficacy study of naltrexone in prevention of opiate relapse among patients who had completed an inpatient treatment program at Merritt Peralta Institute in Oakland. Patients who volunteered for the study were randomly assigned to receive either standard aftercare plus urine testing, or aftercare plus naltrexone and urine testing. Figure 5 (page 80) shows the duration of treatment for the two groups of patients. The data are for only one year because that was the maximum length of a patient's participation in the study.

More of the patients who were receiving naltrexone continued treatment longer than did patients who were in the urine testing group. This is an important finding because retention in treatment is generally associated with improved outcome. In addition, the patients who continued naltrexone were "protected" against relapse to opiate abuse during the time they were regularly ingesting naltrexone.

Several patient characteristics are associated with increased compliance. Upper socioeconomic patients (physicians, attorneys) as a group stayed longer than blue collar workers, and women generally comply better than men.

Figure 5. Retention of subjects in the study

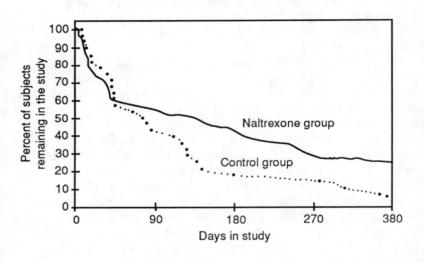

Chapter 6
ENDNOTES

1. M. C. Lee et al., "Duration of Occupancy of Opiate Receptors by Naltrexone," *Journal of Nuclear Medicine* 29, no. 7 (1988): 1207-11.
2. T. Crowley et al., "Naltrexone-Induced Dysphoria in Former Opiate Addicts," *American Journal of Psychiatry,* 142, no. 9 (1985): 1081-84. L. E. Hollister et al.,

"Aversive Effects on Naltrexone in Subjects Not Dependent on Opiates," *Drug and Alcohol Dependence* 8, no. 1 (1981): 37-41. B. A. Judson, and A. Goldstein, "Symptoms Complaints of Patients Maintained on Methadone, LAAM, and Naltrexone at Different Times in Their Addiction Careers," *Drug and Alcohol Dependence* 10, no. 2-3 (1982): 269-82.

7
RELAPSE, RELAPSE PREVENTION, AND RECOVERY

The terms *relapse, relapse prevention,* and *recovery* have no precise meaning. The meanings differ depending on the context of their use, and the differences are of more than academic importance. Differing definitions of these terms cause much controversy in the substance abuse treatment field.

The treatment modality and the goal of treatment can both affect one's view of relapse. For some methadone maintenance patients, the only realistic treatment goal is *reduction* of illicit drug use. Relapse in such patients generally refers to resumption of *addictive use* or the return to drug use of the *same intensity* as in the past. For patients who are in drug-free recovery-oriented treatment, on the other hand, relapse means a return to *any* psychoactive drug use.

Researchers conducting treatment outcome studies usually define relapse in terms that can be quantified. They may, for example, define relapse as *daily* drug use for a specified number of sequential days (for example, daily use for one week); or they may define *relapse* as a consequence of the drug use, such as the return to the hospital for further drug abuse treatment.

Given such differences in definition about a concept so basic to drug abuse treatment, it should come as no surprise that clinicians often have difficulty agreeing with or even communicating with one another.

Clinicians have diverse views about the *cause* of relapse. These differences are significant because clinicians treating opiate abusers choose different treatments depending in part on their beliefs about the cause of relapse.

In this chapter, we review some common ideas about relapse and their application to treatment of the opiate abuser.

RELAPSE RATES

Relapse rates are a ratio, such as the number of subjects treated who relapsed divided by the overall number of subjects treated. Relapse rates, however, are subject to variation depending on the following:

- the definition of relapse used,
- the method used to detect the relapse, and
- the method used to count patients not available for follow-up.

Understanding of relapse rates and the factors that influence them is needed to understand claims of treatment efficacy.

Current Methods of Calculating Relapse Rates

In drug treatment outcome research, a common relapse assessment method uses subject interviews and urine testing to validate current drug use. Family members and other sources of information may also be used to validate information obtained from the patient.

Urine testing would appear to be an objective method of determining relapse; however, this appearance of objectivity is an illusion. Urine testing analytic methods vary in sensitivity, specificity, and in the range of drugs that can be detected. For example, one common method of urine drug screening, EMIT, is very sensitive for morphine, marijuana, and benzoylecgonine (a cocaine metabolite) and can detect their presence in urine for several days following use. Thin layer chromatography (TLC), another commonly used method of urine screening, is less sensitive than EMIT for these drugs, and because TLC is less sensitive, it will not detect some drug use that would have been detected with EMIT.

Two Methods of Measuring Relapse

Two different time frames are commonly used to compute relapse rates. One captures current drug use at a point in time following completion of treatment (for example, one year following treatment). This method is the most *precise* because immediate drug use history can be verified by urinalysis and clinical observation. It is not, however, the most sensitive because treated drug abusers may have periods of drug use interspersed with abstinence. This method of measuring relapse does not capture intermittent drug use unless such use occurs at the time of follow-up.

The second method of measuring relapse attempts to ascertain by history whether drug use occurred *at any time* during the follow-up period. In research studies that present no negative consequence to participants for revealing drug use, some users feel safer in confessing episodes of drug use that have not continued. Thus, relapse rate calculations using this second method are usually higher.

Another important source of relapse rate variation is how patients who could not be contacted for follow-up are counted. Assumptions must be made about subjects lost to follow-up. They may, for example, be counted as relapsed, or replaced by patients who could be located, or not used in the computation at all. In reporting treatment outcome studies, many authors do not specify how they measured or computed the relapse rates, even though each method may lead to different results.

AN OVERVIEW OF RELAPSE MODELS

What causes relapse? Opinions vary. Some attribute relapse to factors in the environment; others attribute relapse to factors within the addict (psychopathology or abnormal metabolism), and still others attribute relapse to a combination or interaction of both. We will first examine metabolic alterations that may be the result of inheritance or chronic exposure to drugs; then we'll consider the impact of the environment and psychopathology.

GENETIC THEORIES AND RELAPSE

Vulnerabilities to drug dependence under genetic control are usually discussed as risk factors to developing addiction, but as diagramed in Figure 6 (page 87), genetic factors may also affect relapse.

Goldstein's Theory

In 1978, Avrum Goldstein hypothesized that some people *inherit* an endorphin deficiency.[1] If people with this deficiency happened to use opiates, they would discover a "normalizing" or euphorogenic effect from the opiate that is greater than experienced by people without the abnormality. This would make opiates more "reinforcing" for them. In effect, opiates would be a "stronger drug" for people with the endorphin deficiency. This would predispose them to develop psychological dependency on opiates, and the memory of the opiate's "normalizing effects" would make it harder for them to remain abstinent after treatment.

Dole and Nyswander's Theory

Before the discovery of narcotic receptors, endorphins, or enkephalins, Dole and Nyswander postulated that repeated exposure to opiate drugs induced metabolic changes in neurons.[2] Methadone corrected or compensated for this metabolic change. Since methadone was meeting a metabolic need of the patient, Dole and Nyswander viewed "replacement therapy" using methadone (perhaps on a lifelong basis) as a rational treatment approach. Methadone maintenance fit the medical model. Giving methadone to an opiate addict was like giving insulin to a diabetic.

Figure 6. Genetic factors and increased vulnerability to relapse

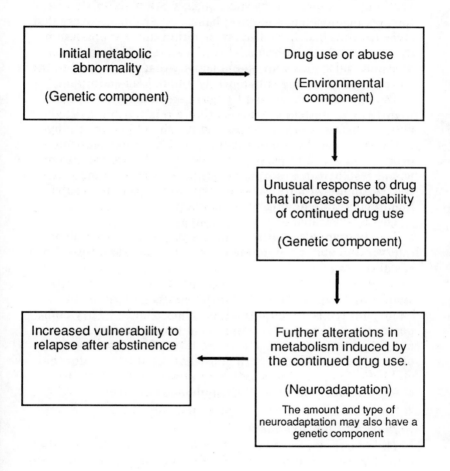

The hypothesis that exposure to opiates produces metabolic alterations is supported by subsequent work with opiate receptors, beta-endorphin, and enkephalins. After the discovery that some neurons had specialized recognition sites for opiates on the neuron cell's membrane, scientists searched for an endogenous substance with opioid activity that would bind to the receptor. Several were subsequently found: beta-endorphin, methionine-enkephalin, and leucine-enkephalin.

In 1978, Goldstein speculated that a relationship existed between beta-endorphin levels and heroin addiction. He hypothesized that the use of heroin would *suppress* endorphin production and that persistent opiate withdrawal symptoms would result from endorphin deficiency. The resulting protracted opiate withdrawal symptom would account for the high relapse rate among opiate addicts.

This is illustrated in Figure 7 (page 89).

The diagram also indicates points of potential treatment intervention and accommodates both biological and psychosocial treatments.

In 1980, Ho and his colleagues published results of their studies that supported Goldstein's hypothesis that beta-endorphin levels are abnormal in opiate addicts.[3] They compared plasma levels of endorphins in heroin addicts and nondrug using controls. The mean level of immunoassayable plasma endorphin activity (a combination of beta-endorphin and beta-lipotropin) was reduced in the heroin addicts to about one-third the level of the nonaddict controls.

Implications for Treatment

The genetic theory of relapse supports the disease model of drug dependence and has pragmatic value for counseling drug abusers. It is a nonjudgmental way to explain to drug abusers why they cannot "control" their use of drugs.

The existence of reduced endorphin levels in heroin addicts provides a plausible physiological reason for relapse. The

Figure 7. Relapse driven by protracted withdrawal symptoms

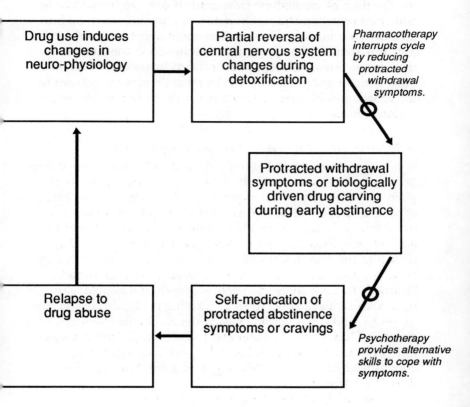

endorphin deficiency model also has an implication regarding the duration of methadone treatment. If one supposes that the addict inherited an endorphin deficiency, analogous to an insulin deficiency in diabetics, then one could argue the need for lifelong replacement. (As previously mentioned in the chapter on methadone maintenance, however, many advocates of methadone maintenance subscribe to the rehabilitative model, not to the genetic model, and therefore reject the notion of lifelong maintenance.)

A Relapse Model Based on Conditioning Theory

In papers published between 1961 and 1973, Abraham Wikler proposed the conditioned *withdrawal syndrome theory* to explain why formerly addicted persons, who appear to be "cured" of their addiction while in treatment or in jail, return to opiate use when no longer physically dependent.[4] He hypothesized that addicts experienced *opiate withdrawal symptoms* when they returned to the neighborhoods in which they had previously experienced opiate withdrawal. In other words, the addicts had "learned" to associate some neighborhoods and people with opiate withdrawal. (This form of learning is called *classical conditioning,* and it may occur outside the conscious awareness of a person.) Thus, environmental and social stimuli formerly associated with actual withdrawal and drug-seeking became classically conditioned stimuli, and they triggered a conditioned withdrawal syndrome.

The model is shown in Figure 8 (page 91).

In 1967, Wikler and Pescor published a description of conditioned withdrawal syndrome in rats.[5] Rats that were no longer morphine dependent showed signs of opiate withdrawal ("wet shakes") when they were returned to the cage where they had previously suffered opiate withdrawal.

In 1980, Sideroff and Jarvik reported instances of conditioned withdrawal in intravenous heroin addicts.[6] Eight heroin addicts who were completing a fourteen-day detoxification

Figure 8. Relapse and environmentally triggered withdrawal

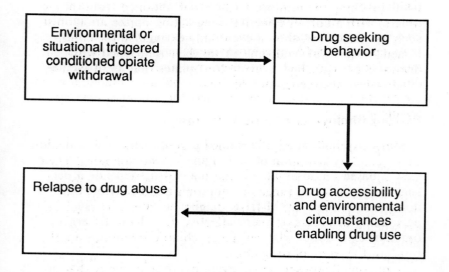

program were shown a six-minute videotape depicting scenes of heroin being prepared for injection and being injected. Compared with a control group of two heroin users who snorted heroin and six patients who were not drug dependent, the intravenous heroin users, while watching the videotape, developed greater increases in anxiety, depression, drug cravings, galvanic skin resistance, and heart rate. These investigators propose that the psychological and physiological changes they observed were produced by conditioned opiate withdrawal.

Implications for Treatment

The conditioning theory of relapse translates to a specific treatment for opiate-dependent individuals. The goal of treatment is to extinguish the conditioned abstinence syndrome. In 1980, Wikler proposed that repeated exposure to stimuli that brought about the conditioned withdrawal syndrome, while blocking the reinforcer (the relief obtained from the opiate) with an orally effective, long-acting opiate antagonist, such as naltrexone, should eventually extinguish the conditioned withdrawal syndrome. After the conditioned withdrawal is extinguished, craving for opiates that are driven by conditioned abstinence should cease.[7]

Psychopathology as a Cause of Relapse

Many psychodynamically trained practitioners view addiction as a secondary symptom of underlying psychopathology. Their view is based on observations that many drug-dependent persons display a broad range of symptoms and behaviors that match one or more DSM-III-R diagnostic categories (such as personality disorders or major affective disorders). Divergent opinions exist about whether the psychiatric symptoms are the *result* or the *cause* of drug abuse.

Some opiate abusers have severe psychopathology that predates their opiate use. In such patients, psychopathology will persist, or may even become more severe, after sustained abstinence from opiates. These patients, often called *dual diagnosis* (that is, a major psychiatric disorder not caused by drug abuse and with a substance abuse disorder), are difficult to treat in traditional substance abuse treatment programs and often do not do well with psychotherapy or other modes of psychiatric treatment. Many bounce back and forth between drug treatment programs and mental health clinics or hospitals, generally creating havoc in both.

Implications for Treatment

The theory that *all* substance abusers have underlying psychopathology has practical ramifications in treatment. Many therapists believe that the patient is self-medicating his or her psychopathology and that the "secondary" symptom of the drug dependency will "disappear" when the underlying psychopathology is adequately treated. As a consequence, they do not confront the drug use during psychotherapeutic or psychopharmacological treatment of the psychopathology.

The therapist can be misled by circular reasoning. When drug abusers are abstinent, it is viewed as evidence that the psychopathology is being resolved; if the drug use resumes or continues, the therapist concludes that the psychopathology has not been resolved.

Most addiction specialists treat the addiction as the *primary problem* and delay treatment of psychopathology until after a period of abstinence. Depression or other psychopathology may be *secondary* to the *drug use* and is often resolved without specific treatment other than that for chemical dependency.

THEORIES OF RECOVERY

Like the term *relapse, recovery* is a term open to different meanings. It can mean cure of addiction, *abstinence* from drug use, or *remission* of the drug-dependent state. Theories about recovery usually describe a process of achieving and maintaining abstinence that is not necessarily related to any specific type of treatment. These theories reflect notions about influences of major life changes in producing and sustaining abstinence.

Winick's Maturation Theory

Using 1955-1960 data from the Federal Bureau of Narcotics Registry, Winick noted that most opiate addicts began use in their late teens and early twenties and then disappeared from the narcotics registry after age thirty-five.[8] From this observation, Winick hypothesized that most opiate addicts "mature out" of the problems that originally lead to heroin use by age thirty-five. After thirty-five years of age, the drive to continue drug use was not sufficiently compelling for them to continue the lifestyle necessary for opiate use.

Although some heroin addicts do mature out of their addiction, many do not. One twenty-year follow-up of fifty-one heroin addicts found that only one was drug-free after age forty.[9] Likewise, Vaillant, who conducted a twenty-year longitudinal study of addicts admitted to the United States Public Health Service Hospital in Lexington, Kentucky in 1952, found that about 35 percent of addicts matured out by age forty.[10]

Natural Recovery from Opiate Addiction

Waldorf studied 201 ex-opiate addicts (half were treated and the other half had quit without treatment).[11] He concluded that "maturing out," "hitting bottom," and existential crises did not entirely explain the variety of recovery experiences. Nor was the ability to quit necessarily related to treatment. Addicts used a variety of methods to obtain and maintain abstinence. Those who were successful generally broke all ties with opiate abusers, developed new interests, new social networks, and new social identities.

Twelve Step Recovery Model

Members of Alcoholic Anonymous or other Twelve Step recovery groups use the term *recovery* to mean more than abstinence from drugs. Being "in recovery" implies the person has accepted addiction as a lifelong, incurable disease; the person is participating in Twelve Step recovery groups; and the person is learning to live a comfortable and responsible life without the use of psychoactive drugs. Additionally, a model of recovery evolving from Twelve Step recovery groups views cessation of drug use as an active, continuing process.

Recovery groups accept that once drug dependence has developed, the illness will persist throughout the remainder of a person's life. Sobriety therefore requires strict abstinence from all psychoactive drugs, aided by continued participation in recovery groups. When Twelve Step recovery group members speak of the quality of peoples' recovery, they mean the number of meetings attended, giving sobriety the highest priority, the level of comfort in living without drugs, and "working" the Steps.

How Twelve Step Groups View Relapse

Because the recovery model stresses abstinence from all mood-altering substances (generally excluding nicotine and caffeine), any use of drugs is called a *relapse*. Behavior may be labeled as "relapse" even before return to drug use. The recovery model stresses that relapse does not happen as a single, isolated event, but is preceded by a period of altered attitudes and thinking. Members of AA refer to this pattern of thinking as "stinking thinking." First, the person might begin to view him- or herself as "cured" and no longer in need of attending meetings or being constantly vigilant to prevent relapse. The person consequently reduces or stops attending AA or other Twelve Step meetings.

Next, the person might question the need to maintain abstinence from *all* psychotropic drugs, and eventually tries a drug, not necessarily the primary drug of abuse, to see if this leads to a compulsive use of the primary drug of abuse. If it does not, it confirms the notion that strict avoidance of all psychoactive drugs is unnecessary.

Finally, the person may be apt to test the ability to control use of the previously abused drug. If loss of control is not immediate, the notion of the "cure" is reinforced, and the person is further estranged from recovery support peers.

Implications for Treatment

Twelve Step recovery incorporates many of the forces of change described by Waldorf in natural recovery: new social networks, new social identity, and new interests. The challenge to substance abuse treatment professionals is in finding ways to engage more patients in Twelve Step recovery, and in creating new ways to harness the many potent forces of change that operate within Twelve Step recovery.

Chapter 7
ENDNOTES

1. A. Goldstein, "Endorphins: Physiology and Clinical Implications," *Annals of the New York Academy of Sciences* 311 (1978): 49-58.
2. V. P. Dole and M. E. Nyswander, "Heroin Addiction: A Metabolic Disease, " *Archives of Internal Medicine* 120, no. 1 (1967): 19-24.
3. W. K. K. Ho, H. L. Wen, and N. Ling, "Beta-endorphine-like Immunoactivity in the Plasma of Heroin Addicts and Normal Subjects," *Neuropharmacology* 19, no. 1 (1980): 117-20.
4. A. Wikler, "On the Nature of Addiction and Habituation," *British Journal of A ddiction* 57 (1961): 73-80. A. Wikler, "Conditioning Factors in Opiate Addiction and Relapse," in *Narcotics,* D. M. Wilner and G. G. Kassebaum, eds. (New York: McGraw Hill, 1965): 85-100. A. Wikler, "Dynamics of Drug Dependence: Implications of a Conditioning Theory for Research and Treatment," in: *Opiate Addiction: Origins and Treatment,* S. Fisher and A. Freedman, eds. (Washington, D.C.: Winston and Sons, 1973): 7-21.
5. A. Wikler and F. T. Pescor, "Classical Conditioning of a Morphine Abstinence Phenomenon, Reinforcement of Opioid-Using Behavior and 'Relapse' in Morphine-Addicted Rats," *Psychopharmacologia* 10 (1967): 255-84.
6. S. I. Sideroff and M. E. Jarvik, "Conditioned Responses to a Videotape Showing Heroin-Related Stimili,"

International Journal of the Addictions 15, no. 4 (1980): 529-36.

7. A. Wikler, "A Theory of Opioid Dependence," in: *Theories on Drug Abuse: Selected Contemporary Perspectives,* D. Lettieri, M. Sayers, and H. Pearson, eds. (Washington, D.C.: National Institute on Drug Abuse Research Monograph #30. DHHS Pub. No. ADM 80-967, 1980), 174-78.

8. C. Winick, "Maturing out of Narcotic Addiction," *Bulletin on Narcotics* 41, no.1 (1962): 1-7.

9. P. Harrington and T. A. Cox, "A Twenty-Year Follow-Up of Narcotic Addicts in Tuscon, Arizona," *American Journal of Drug and Alcohol Abuse* (126), no. 1 (1979): 25-37.

10. G. E. Vaillant, "A 20-Year Follow-Up of New York Narcotic Addicts, " *Archives of General Psychiatry* 29, no. 2 (1973): 237-41.

11. D. Waldorf, "Natural Recovery from Opiate Addiction: Some Social-Psychological Processes of Untreated Recovery," *Journal of Drug Issues* 13, no. 2 (1983): 237-80.

APPENDIX

THE TWELVE STEPS OF
ALCOHOLICS ANONYMOUS*

1. We admitted we were powerless over alcohol — that our lives had become unmanageable.
2. Came to believe that a Power greater than ourselves could restore us to sanity.
3. Made a decision to turn our will and our lives over to the care of God *as we understood Him.*
4. Made a searching and fearless moral inventory of ourselves.
5. Admitted to God, to ourselves, and to another human being the exact nature of our wrongs.
6. Were entirely ready to have God remove all these defects of character.
7. Humbly asked Him to remove our shortcomings.
8. Made a list of all persons we had harmed, and became willing to make amends to them all.
9. Made direct amends to such people wherever possible, except when to do so would injure them or others.
10. Continued to take personal inventory and when we were wrong promptly admitted it.
11. Sought through prayer and meditation to improve our conscious contact with God *as we understood Him,* praying only for knowledge of His will for us and the power to carry that out.
12. Having had a spiritual awakening as the result of these steps, we tried to carry this message to alcoholics, and to practice these principles in all our affairs.

---

* The Twelve Steps are from *Alcoholics Anonymous* (Third Edition), published by AA World Services, Inc., New York, N.Y., 59-60. Reprinted with permission.

GLOSSARY

Editor's Note: Many of these terms are not used in the text, but are terms commonly used in the discussion of opiate addiction.

BLUE THUNDER. Name of a form of heroin, probably originated from a thirty-nine-foot, 900-horsepower boat that U.S. Customs uses off the coast of Florida to interdict drug smuggling speedboats (*see also* P-Dope).

BOOSTING. Refers to increasing the psychotropic effect of methadone or other narcotic by simultaneously ingesting another drug such as a diazepam.[1]

CHASING THE DRAGON. Smoking opium. Also the title of a book about opium smoking in Hong Kong.

CHINA WHITE. The term was originally used to refer to a pure form of heroin from Southeast Asia. Since 1980, it has also been used to refer to mixtures containing fentanyl.

DENIAL. Refers to a patient's inability to acknowledge the connection between his or her drug use and lifestyle. Drug abusers may attribute relationship breakups, loss of jobs, and unpleasant feelings to causes other than the drug use. They often point to life adversity (which a drug abuse counselor would recognize as a *consequence* of drug use) as the *reason* for drug use. This misattribution is denial if the patient, for psychological reasons, is unable to see the relationship.

Denial is often incorrectly used to mean "lying." For example, the patient denies having more than two beers per day. The use of the term *denial* is incorrect if the patient knows that the number of beers consumed is greater, but knowingly misrepresents his consumption.

FOURS AND DOORS. A combination of codeine (#4) and glutethimide (Doriden) that is taken orally by opiate addicts as a substitute for heroin. The combination was first noted in the medical literature in 1969.[2] Because glutethimide is a potent sleeping pill that produces respiratory depression, overdoses and fatalities can occur.[3]

GOLDEN CRESENT. A term referring to the opium-producing areas in Southwest Asia in Pakistan, Afghanistan and Iran.

GOLDEN TRIANGLE. A term referring to the opium-producing areas of Southeast Asia in Burma, Laos, and Thailand.

H. Heroin.

HORSE. Heroin.

LAAM (Levo-Alpha-Acetyl Methadol). A narcotic similar to methadone, but longer acting. LAAM can be administered every other day.

LOADS. Glutethimide and codeine (*see also* fours and doors).

NARCOTIC. Any addictive drug that dulls the senses, relieves pain, and induces sleep. A narcotic generally refers to an opiate, but is sometimes used to refer to other illicit drugs.

NARCOTICS ANONYMOUS (NA). An organization formed in 1951 to assist opiate dependent persons in their recovery from opiate addiction. NA is modeled after Alcoholics Anonymous.

NATIONAL CLEARINGHOUSE FOR DRUG ABUSE INFORMATION. The publication distribution branch of the National

Institute on Drug Abuse (NIDA). Single copies of NIDA research monographs and other publications can be obtained by writing to the National Clearinghouse for Drug Abuse Information, Box 416, Kensington, MD 20795.

OBSESSION. See P-Dope.

OPIUM WARS. Two wars waged by England against the Imperial Government of China to allow importation of opium into China. Opium was grown in India and Persia and first transported to China by the British East India Company, and later by ships of the American Clipper Trade. The first Opium War (1839-1842) ended with the defeat of China. The British negotiated the Treaty of Nanking, which, among other concessions, ceded Hong Kong to the British and opened five other coastal cities in China where the British could have homes and consulates, and carry on trade under a fixed tariff of 5 percent. The second Opium War (1856-1860) gave Great Britain, France, and other countries access to ten more ports in China, the right to navigate the Yangtze River, and to travel throughout China.

P-DOPE. A street term for "pure dope," a form of heroin first noted in New Jersey in December 1985. By 1987, P-Dope, sold under street names of "Obsession" and "Blue Thunder," was being sold in Connecticut. The purity of P-Dope ranges from 50 to 96 percent heroin.[4]

SAODAP. The Special Action Office On Drug Abuse Prevention was established in 1972 as a temporary executive branch office to reduce drug abuse in the United States. It preceded the National Institute on Drug Abuse. It was disbanded and its activities passed to NIDA at the end of 1974.

SEDATIVE-HYPNOTICS. Refers to a functional category of alcohol and other drugs, which include barbiturates, benzodiazepines, methaqualone, and buspirone. Synonyms include "minor tranquilizers" and "sleeping pills."

SMACK. Another word for *heroin*.

T'S AND BLUES. A combination of *Talwin* and the antihistamine tripelennamine (manufactured as *blue* tablets), that is injected intravenously as a heroin substitute. T's and Blues are most frequently abused in the midwestern United States.

To prevent I.V. use of Talwin, Winthrop Laboratories added naloxone to the tablet in 1983 (brand name Talwin Nx). Naloxone is a narcotic antagonist that is poorly absorbed from the stomach. Naloxone should have no effect when the tablet is taken orally, but will block some of the effects of pentazocine if the tablet is dissolved and injected. T's and Blues continue to be abused,[5] but at a much decreased level.[6]

Glossary
ENDNOTES

1. M. L. Stitzer et al., "Diazepam Use Among Methadone Maintenance Patients: Patterns and Dosage," *Drug and Alcohol Dependence* 8, no. 3 (1981): 189-99.
2. C. A. Shamoian and A. K. Shapiro, "Abuse of an Euphoretic Combination," appeared as a letter in the *Journal of the American Medical Association* 207, no. 3 (1969): 1919.
3. D. N. Bailey and R. F. Shaw, "Blood Concentration and Clinical Findings in Nonfatal and Fatal Intoxication Involving Glutethimide and Codeine," *Journal of Toxicology. Clinical Toxicology* 23, no. 7-8 (1985-86): 557-70.
4. "New, Purer Heroin Possible Cause of Connecticut Deaths," *National Institute on Drug Abuse Notes* (Winter 1987-1988): 24-25.

5. D. A. Reed, and S. H. Schnoll, "Abuse of Pentazocine-Naloxone Combination," *Journal of the American Medical Association* 256, no. 18 (1986): 2562-64.

6. W. R. True et al., "Pentazocine-Naloxone Experimenters Among Abusers of Pentazocine and Tripelennamine from a V. A. Treatment Population," *International Journal of the Addictions* 22, no. 2 (1988): 217-26.

SUGGESTED READING

Agar, M. *Ripping and Running: A Formal Ethnography of Urban Heroin Addicts.* New York: Seminar Press, 1973.

Berridge, V., and G. Edwards. *Opium and the People.* New Haven, Conn.: Yale University Press, 1987.

Brecher, E. M. ed. *Licit and Illicit Drugs.* Boston: Little, Brown and Co., 1972.

Bresler, F. S. *The Chinese Mafia.* New York: Stein and Day, 1981.

Burroughs, W. *Junky.* Baltimore: Penguin Books, 1953.

_____ . *Naked Lunch.* New York: Grove Press, 1966.

Carriel, D. *So Fair a House: The Story of Synanon.* Englewood Cliffs, N.J.: Prentice-Hall, 1963.

Chein, I. *The Road to H.* New York: Basic Books, 1964.

Courtwright, D. T. *Dark Paradise: Opiate Addiction in America Before 1940.* Cambridge, Mass.: Harvard University Press, 1982.

De Leon, G., and J. T. Ziegenfuss. *Therapeutic Communities for Addictions: Readings in Theory, Research and Practice.* Springfield, Ill.: Charles C. Thomas, 1986.

Eddy, N. B. *The National Research Council Involvement in the Opiate Problem 1928-1971.* Washington, D.C.: National Academy of Sciences, 1973.

Endore, G. *Synanon.* Garden City, N.Y.: Doubleday, 1967.

Hanson, W., and G. Beschner, et al. *Life with Heroin: Voices from the Inner City.* Lexington, Mass.: Lexington Books, 1985.

Inciardi, J. A. *The War on Drugs: Heroin, Cocaine, Crime, and Public Policy.* Palo Alto, Calif.: Mayfield Publishing Company, 1986.

Kaplan, J. *The Hardest Drug: Heroin and Public Policy.* Chicago: University of Chicago Press, 1983.

Kirsch, M. M. *Designer Drugs*. Minneapolis: CompCare Publications, 1986.

Kolb, L. *Drug Addiction: A Medical Problem*. Springfield, Ill.: Charles C. Thomas, 1962.

Lewin, L. *Phantastica: Narcotic and Stimulating Drugs*. Translation by P.H.A. Wirth. London: Routledge and Kegan Paul, 1964.

Lindersmith, A. R. *Addiction and Opiates*. Chicago: Aldine Publishing Co., 1965.

McCoy, A. W. *The Politics of Heroin in Southeast Asia*. New York: Harper and Row, 1972.

Murray, T. H., W. Gaylin, and R. Macklin. *Feeling Good and Doing Better: Ethics and Non-therapeutic Drug Use*. Clifton, N.J.: The Humana Press, 1984.

Musto, D. F. *The American Disease: Origins of Narcotic Control*. New Haven, Conn.: Yale University Press, 1973.

O'Brien, R., and S. Cohen. *The Encyclopedia of Drug Abuse*. New York: Facts on File, 1984.

Rachal, P. *Federal Narcotic Enforcement: Reorganization and Reform*. Boston: Auburn House Publishing Company, 1982.

Ray, O. S. *Drugs, Society, and Human Behavior*. St. Louis: C. V. Mosby, 1972.

Rosenbaum, M. *Women on Heroin*. New Brunswick, N. J.: Rutgers University Press, 1981.

Seymour, R., D. Smith, D. Inaba, and M. Landry. *The New Drugs: Look-Alikes, Drugs of Deception, and Designer Drugs*. Center City, Minn.: Hazelden Educational Materials, 1989.

Shulgin, A. T. *The Controlled Substances Act: A Resource Manual of the Current Status of the Federal Drug Laws*. Lafayette, Calif.: Alexander T. Shulgin, 1988.

Smith, D. E., and G. R. Gay, eds. *It's So Good, Don't Even Try It Once*. Englewood Cliffs, N.J.: Prentice-Hall, 1972.

Trebach, A. S. *The Heroin Solution*. New Haven, Conn.: Yale University Press, 1982.

Waldorf, D. *Careers in Dope.* Englewood Cliffs, N.J.:
  Prentice-Hall, 1973.
Walker, W. O., III. *Drug Control in the Americas.* Albuquer-
  que: University of New Mexico Press, 1981.
Yablonsky, L. *The Tunnel Back: Synanon.* New York: Macmil-
  lan, 1965.

INDEX

A

Abstinence, 10
Acetaminophen, 21, 56
Addiction, neurobiology of,
    13-14
Addiction Severity Index, 27
AIDS, 6, 67;
    and drug abuse, 12-13;
    in methadone maintenance
    programs, 63.
AIDS Commission
    of 1988, 13
Alcoholics Anonymous, 3-4,
    10-11, 28, 36, 39, 41, 94-95
Alcoholism, 3;
    as a leading cause of death
    in methadone
    maintenance programs, 11
Alprazolam, 33
American Medical
    Association, 3, 13
American Medical Society
    for the Treatment of
    Alcoholism and Other
    Drug Dependencies, 13
Amphetamines, 5-6
Antabuse, 33
Assessment,
    of dependence, 27-31

B

Brain cells, 45;
    cell communication, 46-47;
    neuroadaptation in during

opiate use, 45, 47;
    noradrenergic, 45, 47

C

California Department of
    Alcohol and Drug Abuse,
    67
California Department of
    Health Services, 35
Chemical Dependency
    Recovery Hospitals, 35
Chemical Dependency
    Treatment, 34-36
China White, 24
Chlordiazepoxide, 33
Chlorpromazine, 51
Classical conditioning, 90
Clonidine detoxification,
    13, 53;
    in treatment of opiate
    withdrawal, 55-57;
    side effects of, 56
Clonidine transdermal patch,
    53-54
Cocaine:
    abuse of, 6;
    free-basing, 5
Comprehensive Crime
    Control Act of 1984, 24
Controlled Substances Act, 23
Controlled Substance Analog
    Enforcement Act
    of 1986, 24

D

Darvocet, 23
Darvon, 22-23, 51;
    dependence on, 58
Daytop Lodge, 3, 42
Dederick, Charles, 2, 41
Demerol, 1, 5
Designer drugs, 23
Designer opiates, 6, 23-24
Detoxification, 45-46;
    principles of, 50-51
Diagnostic and Statistical
    Manual of Mental
    Disorders Third Edition,
    Revised (DSM-III-R), 8,
    13, 92
Diazepam, 33, 51
Dilaudid, 20
Documentation:
    of addiction, 68;
    of physical dependence, 68
Dole, Dr. Vincent, 61-63, 86
Dole and Nyswander's
    Theory, 86
Drug Enforcement
    Administration, 12, 19, 24
Drug-free:
    philosophy, 11;
    recovery, 10;
    treatment, 33-34
Dual diagnosis, 92
DuPont Pharmaceuticals, 77

E

Ecstasy, 23
EMIT:
    method of urine testing, 84
Endorphins, 17

F

Federal Bureau of Narcotics
    Registry, 93
Federation of Dutch Junkie
    Leagues, 7
Fentanyl, 1, 5, 21-22
Food and Drug
    Administration, 12, 53,
    65-67, 70, 74, 77

G

Gitlow, Dr. Stanley, 40;
    Gitlow's "rule of ten," 40
Goldstein, Avrum, 86, 89
Goldstein's Theory, 86

H

Haight-Ashbury, the, 4
Haight-Ashbury Free
    Medical Clinics, 12, 50
Harrison Narcotic Act, 2
Heroin, 19-20
    becoming acceptable in
    some subcultures, 5;
    dependence, 1;
    in the Vietnam War, 4;
    secondary dependence
    on, 5;
    use in other countries, 7
Heroin addicts:
    and crime, 5;
    society's obligation to, 4;
    stereotypes of, 1

HIV infection:
  and intravenous
  drug use, 6;
  and methadone
  maintenance, 63. *See
  also* AIDS
Hydromorphone, 20
Hypodermic needle:
  introduction of, 2

I

Ibuprofen, 56
Innovar, 21
Intravenous injection, 5

J

Joint Commission on
  Accreditation of
  Hospitals, 11
Jones, Maxwell, 41
Jung, Carl, 41

L

Librium, 33

M

Maximum strength, 17-18
MDA, 23
MDMA, 23
Mendocino Family, 42
Merritt Peralta Institute,
  54, 79
Meperidine, 1, 5, 21
Methadone, 22;
  government regulations
  and, 11, 68-69;

in treatment of opiate
  withdrawal, 51-53, 57-58
Methadone Maintenance, 1;
  as a treatment modality, 3,
  10;
  criteria for admission into,
  65-67;
  inpatient, 52;
  in the 1980s, 6;
  long term, 52;
  models of, 62-64;
  origins of, 61-62;
  outpatient, 52;
  poor candidates for, 28;
  regulation of, 11;
  screening patients for,
  64-65;
  short term, 52
  treatment phases, 69-74
Mid City Consortium, 12
Milligram strength, 17-18
Mixed opiate/sedative-
  hypnotic dependence, 56
Morphine, 5
Motrin, 56

N

Naloxone, 17, 68
Naltrexone, 1, 13;
  use in treating opiate
  dependency, 77-80
Narcan, 17
Narcotic addiction:
  treatment of before 1960, 2
Narcotics Anonymous, 3,
  10-11, 28, 36-37, 39, 71, 73

Synanon, 3, 41-42
Synthetics, 19

T
Talwin, 17;
  dependence on, 58
Temgesic, 17
Therapeutic Communities, 2;
  first wave, 41-42;
  second wave, 42-43;
  third wave, 43;
  as a treatment modality, 10
Thorazine, 51
Thunder Road, 42
TLC:
  as a type of urine testing,
  84
Treatment phases:
  first phase, 69-70;
  fourth phase, 73-74;
  second phase, 71;
  third phase, 72-73
Trexan, 77
Twelve Steps, The, 38
Twelve Step Programs, 28,
  34, 40, 71, 73, 95
Twelve Step Recovery
  Process, 33, 39, 94-96
Tylox, 21
Tylenol, 21, 56

U
United States Public Health
  Service Hospital, 94

V
Valium, 33, 51
Veteran's Administration, 42
Vicodan, 21
Vietnam War, the, 4, 18

W
Walden House, 42
Wilson, Bill, 41
Wikler, Abraham, 90
Winick's Maturation Theory,
  93-94
Withdrawal:
  pharmocological treatment
  of, 51-59;
  relationship of withdrawal
  symptoms to narcotic
  use, 48;
  symptoms of, 49
Withdrawal Syndrome
  Theory, 90

X
Xanax, 33